SCINTILLA

The Journal of the Vaughan Association

19

The *Peripatetickes* look on *God*, as they do on *Carpenters*,
who build with *stone* and *timber*, without any *infusion* of *life*.
But the *world*, which is *God's building*, is full of *Spirit*, *quick*,
and *living*.

> Thomas Vaughan.
> *Anthroposophia Theomagica.*

With what deep murmurs through times silent stealth
Doth thy transparent, cool and watry wealth
> Here flowing fall,
> And chide, and call . . .

> Henry Vaughan,
> 'The Water-fall'.

A journal of literary criticism, prose and new poetry
in the metaphysical tradition

Published by
The Vaughan Association

Published in 2016
Scintilla is a publication of The Vaughan Association

Some of the essays in each issue of *Scintilla* originate in talks first given at
The Vaughan Association's annual Colloquium held over the last full weekend in April
near the Vaughans' birth-place at Newton Farm near Llansantffraed, Breconshire.

ISBN-13: 978-1530307180
ISBN-10: 153030718X
ISSN 1368-5023

Published with the financial support of the Welsh Books Council

General Editor, Dr. Joseph Sterrett
Poetry Editors, Prof. Damian Walford Davies and Prof. Kevin Mills
Prose Editor, Prof. Erik Ankerberg

Art Work:
Featured photographs are by Christopher Werrett.
The editors wish to thank him for permission to reproduce his work.

Typeset in Wales by the Dinefwr Press
Rawlings Road, Llandybïe, Carmarthenshire, SA18 3YD
Printed by CreateSpace, USA

Dedicated to the memory of
Peter Thomas
16 January 1935 – 18 September 2014

Contents

Preface

In *Scintilla 19* we celebrate the memory of Peter Thomas who, along with Anne Cluysenaar, organised the first Colloquium in 1995, which led both to The Vaughan Association and *Scintilla* as a journal. Peter's work as a scholar of seventeenth-century literature, his sharp eye, dry wit, and congenial, curious, welcoming approach all combined with his deft skill as an editor to leave a legacy that will be unrivalled, not only in the journal itself, but in the enthusiasm of a community interested in the Vaughans and their poetic legacy. This issue appropriately opens with an insightful and beautiful study by Robert Wilcher, a long-time friend of Peter's, of Henry Vaughan's public and private elegies. Several of these poems can be dated to the years immediately after the death of Henry's younger brother, William, who died following his participation in the royalist uprising in South Wales during 1648. They give a glimpse of Henry's sense of deep personal loss and the psychological, spiritual terrain he traverses in his 'work of mourning' while acknowledging that 'he is left with only "the snuff" of the candle that once burned brightly'. They perform, to use Stevie Davies's phrase, a kind of 'self-therapy'. But, Wilcher reminds us, Henry's poems of mourning go beyond the personal, extending their sense of grief into the politics of the moment by giving voice to 'the traumatized condition of the royalist remnant in its darkest hour'.

It is these combined political, personal and spiritual energies that the Vaughan brothers have so often excited in the pages of *Scintilla*. Identical twins, shaped by their Breconshire birthplace with its reassuring beauty, Henry and Thomas both articulated their memories of the Usk river valley with its hills and groves, creatures, herbs, stones, history and myths. This magical landscape asserted itself in their imaginations even as they experienced the trauma of enormous social and political change. Their experience of civil wars, regicide and republican revolution, the loss of familiar church and state institutions, and the discontinuity and alienation that resulted, all imprinted on their work. As the twins reinvented themselves, Henry as 'Silurist' and Thomas as 'Eugenius Philalethes', they explored the connections between identity, adversity and the creative process in their writing. *Scintilla* exists to probe these conjunctions, crossing boundaries between past and present, between place and vision, our physical environment and our inner lives, between metaphysical experiences and the language of science, poetry, and healing.

Henry Vaughan is the focus of the next two articles as well. Joseph Ashmore explores Henry's visual recreation of biblical places, which is an aspect of his poetry that has implications for its importance as a focus for spiritual meditation. Ashmore offers a valuable correction to Barbara Lewalski's assertion that Protestant meditation, for fear of idolatry, rejected poetry that 'stimulated the senses' and offered 'sensuous immediacy'; the two were not always connected, Ashmore states. Offering readings of 'The Mount of Olives', 'Ascension-day', and 'The Search' as examples, Ashmore asserts that Vaughan, like Herbert before him, 'provides an alternative, poetic structure for finding God'. As

9

Wilcher does to a degree, Jonathan Nauman ties Vaughan's poetic strategies to his engagement with the restrictive religious policies of the Puritan government during the Interregnum. Comparing Vaughan's 'Christ's Nativity' to George Herbert's 'Christmas', Nauman offers a rich reading of the poems that preserves a careful Protestant concern with continued life given to pagan rituals in holiday festivities, while at the same time interrogating Puritan authorities for their castigation of holiday festivals. Vaughan offers a literary performance of Christmas celebration that, Nauman argues, seeks to preserve a 'sense of surrounding holiness in the external world' in traditional worship.

During the last years with Peter was editor, *Scintilla's* remit widened to include the wider metaphysical tradition. It had really been an implicit aspect of the journal from the start underscored most clearly by the desire to cross the creative / critical divide by celebrating new poetry. There was also a particular interest in scholarship that looked at poets leading up to and during the seventeenth century such as Robert Southwell, George Herbert, Thomas Traherne, even on occasion William Shakespeare, not to mention more contemporary examples such as R.S. Thomas and Rowan Williams. Joseph Sterrett contributes an essay to this issue which had been a topic of discussion between he and Peter for some time: a poem by a seldom-discussed welsh – or, at least Marcher – metaphysical poet, John Davies of Hereford, commemorating the King of Denmark's state visit to the court of James I in 1606. Davies himself is in many ways an example of the mobile and flexible identities that had become possible at the time, a flexibility already noted in the Vaughan brothers. Sterrett draws a small but distinct connection between Davies's poetic strategies and the moment Shakespeare decides to depict a similar meeting of kings at the start one of his last play, *Henry VIII* or *All is True*. Moving to the very recent past, Jeremy Hooker also analyses the dynamic between two poets, this time Anne Cluysenaar and Henry Vaughan. Hooker's reflections trace the inspiration Cluysenaar took from the struggles Vaughan experienced some 300 years before. This 'conversation' illuminates her own experience, her 'vulnerability' and 'agony over the disgraces of the age', 'her exploratory art, and her personal relationships' as she engages in the act of becoming herself, 'Matter watching itself', 'becoming self-conscious'.

Cluysenaar's *Vaughan Variations* were born, Hooker reminds us, out of her sensitivity to the horrific suffering involved in the Balkan conflict in the 1990s. The new poems that have earned their place in this volume of *Scintilla* arise out of a similar awareness. They challengingly embody the paradoxes involved in living in what Graham Hartill calls life's 'field of harm'. As this volume goes to press, that phrase conjures the obscenities of the Syrian conflict, attended by the killing waters of the eastern Aegean with their pitiful refugee rafts. It also – responsibly, and without falling foul of a category error – applies (in different forms) to aspects of lives lived in ostensibly safe environments, as our poets convincingly demonstrate.

The poems – all tightly articulated and conceptually driven – engage with the ways in which (in the words of Maria Apichella) 'The night is present' in the midst of all our blessings, and how our rites seek to fend off what Hartill smartly distils as 'the fangs!' What is offered here are personal and contemporary versions of 'Dante's wood', 'Wilfred Owen's profound dull tunnel', 'Eliot's London Bridge', and 'Hansel and Gretel's European forest'

– overlaid with all the mythopoeic resonances that those constructs bring with them. In tune with the spirit of this journal, the poems included in *Scintilla 19* avoid the simplicities of dogma and are careful to locate themselves in ambiguous terrain – a cairn chamber that is a site of both death and rebirth, 'mirror-world[s]', domestic hearth-space that is also profoundly unsettling. They walk a tightrope (the subject of Matthew Barton's 'Balancing Act') between scepticism and openness. In doing so, they are all the more alive to the world's physical and spiritual ecologies of light and dark.

Henry Vaughan's
Public and Private Elegies

ROBERT WILCHER

To his family and friends, the death of Peter Thomas has been felt as a deeply personal loss. Those of us who looked forward to meeting him each year at the Vaughan colloquium in Breconshire have mourned his passing in quiet moments of reflection upon the warmth and generosity of mind that made him such a genial companion. But Dr Peter Thomas was also a public figure, whose many achievements – as university teacher and supervisor of research, literary historian and critic, and editor of *Scintilla* – did so much to illuminate and communicate his enthusiasm for the writing of the seventeenth century. It is a privilege to contribute to this memorial volume and pay tribute to both the human qualities and the professional rigour that he brought to his devoted advocacy of the work of Henry and Thomas Vaughan over the past twenty years in the UVVA. My topic has been chosen to reflect the two dimensions of loss that so many of his friends and admirers have been slowly coming to terms with since his death.

———————

I

Let me set the scene for what I want to say about Vaughan's elegies with a comment by Alan Rudrum: 'No other period of English literature has surpassed the poems of mourning of the early seventeenth century; and while most readers will doubtless feel that no one poem of Vaughan's can challenge King's "Exequy" or Milton's "Lycidas", few other poets of the period produced so large a body of splendid verse in that kind as he did.'[1] The mention of 'poems of mourning' as a literary 'kind' raises the issue of definition and the two examples cited by Rudrum go to the heart of the distinction between private

---

1 Alan Rudrum, 'Henry Vaughan's Poems of Mourning' in *Of Paradise and Light: Essays on Henry Vaughan and John Milton in Honor of Alan Rudrum*, ed. Donald R. Dickson and Holly Faith Nelson (Newark: University of Delaware Press, 2004), p. 309.

and public articulations of the experience of bereavement that I wish to explore in this essay. In its origins in ancient Greece, as Peter Sacks explains, the term 'elegy' denoted verses composed in alternating dactylic hexameters and pentameters accompanied by a flute; although they could contain 'a fairly broad range of topics', from martial epigrams to amatory complaints, behind this variety of subject matter 'there may have lain an earlier, more exclusive association of the flute song's elegiacs with the expression of grief'. The 'miscellaneous approach to content' continued in Latin adaptations of the elegiac form, but with 'an increasingly intense focus on the amatory complaint'. During the sixteenth century in England, however, the elegy came to be associated more and more with the expression of mortal loss and consolation; and by the seventeenth century, two distinct branches had evolved into private poems like Henry King's expression of a very personal grief at the loss of his wife in January 1623/4 and public poems like Thomas Carew's assessment of the impact on the literary world of John Donne's demise in 1633.[2]

King wrote a good many elegies of the second kind – on the deaths of Prince Henry, Sir Walter Raleigh, John Donne, Gustavus Adolphus, and Charles I, as well as other less exalted men and women – but the opening lines of 'The Exequy' indicate a significant difference between such formal statements of public loss and his grief-stricken meditation at the grave of a beloved companion:

> Accept, thou Shrine of my Dead Saint!
> Instead of Dirges this Complaint;
> And, for sweet flowres to crowne thy Hearse,
> Receive a strew of weeping verse
> From thy griev'd Friend; whome Thou might'st see
> Quite melted into Teares for Thee.[3]

Unlike the personal focus of a complaint, the dirge performed a social or political function, often marked by the use of first person plural pronouns: speaking on behalf of the intellectual elite of Caroline England, for example, King admits that 'wee can never pay' the debt owed to 'Dr. Donne Deane of Paules', who lent 'our Age such summes of witt'; and 'A Deepe Groane, fetch'd at the Funerall of . . . Charles the First' begins on a note of general mourning –

---

2 See Peter M. Sacks, *The English Elegy: Studies in the Genre from Spenser to Yeats* (Baltimore and London: The Johns Hopkins University Press, 1987 (1985)), pp. 2-3; and Antoon Van Velzen, 'Two Versions of the Funeral Elegy: Henry King's "The Exequy" and Thomas Carew's ". . . Elegie upon . . . Donne"', *Comitatus: A Journal of Medieval and Renaissance Studies* 15 (1984), 45-57.

3 'An Exequy To his Matchlesse never to be forgotten Friend', *The Poems of Henry King*, ed. Margaret Crum (Oxford: Clarendon Press, 1965), p. 68.

> To speake our Griefes at full over Thy Tombe
> (Great Soul) we should be Thunder-struck, and dumbe:
> The trivial Off'rings of our bubling eyes
> Are but faire Libels at such Obsequies –

and starts its peroration by proclaiming the royalist community's fealty to the dead king's heir: 'Thus Thou our Martyr died'st: but Oh! we stand / A Ransome for another Charles his Hand.'[4] The poet as an individual, nursing his grief in private at the graveside of his wife, can freely confess to being 'melted into Teares', whereas such 'trivial Off'rings' are out of place in the public 'Obsequies' of a great monarch, whose loss transcends indulgence in mere personal sorrow.

II

Several of Henry Vaughan's elegies fall into the public category: two are tributes to friends who died in the civil wars; two record the passing of men who had served the state in local offices – his cousin, Charles Walbeoffe, a Justice of the Peace, who died in 1653, and Arthur Trevor, a judge on the Brecon circuit, who died in January 1666/7.[5] In paying tribute to their characters and achievements, Vaughan adopted conventions that had come down from the funeral elegies and epitaphs of antiquity, but with an added element of political partisanship that was inevitable given the situation of a poet who was stubbornly committed to a defeated cause and an outlawed church. For example, he concludes the elegy for a young comrade killed in battle towards the end of the first civil war with the hope that his lines will 'to the faith of better times commend / Thy loyal upright life, and gallant end'; and three years later, he writes as spokesman for a beleaguered royalist community and looks forward to a reward in heaven for the 'fair and open valour' and the '*piety* and *learning*' that graced the person of another casualty of the fight against the Puritan rebels.[6]

The most compelling and sophisticated of Vaughan's secular elegies is the fine tribute to his cousin, whose acceptance of office under the Parliamentary authorities in Brecon had been frowned upon by some of those loyal to the defeated monarchy. The poet begins with a contrast between the empty show of the civic dignitaries who attended the funeral and his own genuine grief:

4 *Poems of Henry King*, pp. 77, 110, 116.

5 The first two were published in *Olor Iscanus* (1651) and the other two in *Thalia Rediviva* (1678).

6 'An Elegy on the Death of Mr R.W. Slain in the Late Unfortunate Differences at Rowton Heath, near Chester, 1645'; 'An Elegy on the Death of Mr R. Hall, Slain at Pontefract, 1648', in *Henry Vaughan: The Complete Poems*, ed. Alan Rudrum (Harmondsworth: Penguin Books, [1976] 1983), pp. 81-4, 91-3.

Now, that the public sorrow doth subside,
And those slight tears which *custom* springs, are dried;
While all the rich & *outside mourners* pass
Home from thy *dust* to empty their own *glass:*
I (who the throng affect not, nor their state:)
Steal to thy grave undressed, to meditate
On our sad loss, accompanied by none,
An obscure mourner that would weep alone.

The pronouns in the phrases 'their state' and 'our sad loss' announce Vaughan's political affiliations and the last line leads the reader to expect a personal 'complaint' rather than a ceremonial 'dirge' for the dead man. But the troubling circumstances of Walbeoffe's career during the interregnum compel the poet to adopt a more public stance in what follows. Determined to be the 'just recorder' of his cousin's 'death and worth', he defends his conduct as a 'virtuous' servant of the local community even when engulfed politically by 'such mists, that none could see his way':

When private interest did all hearts bend
And wild dissents the public peace did rend:
Thou neither won, nor worn wert still thy self;
Not awed by force, nor basely bribed by pelf.

Even 'bad laws' were turned 'to good' in his hands, because he looked towards the 'glory' of heaven rather than seeking 'to lord it here' and was tempted by 'no bribes, nor fees / Our new oppressors' best annuities'. Having vindicated Walbeoffe's public life, Vaughan turns to his heart – 'Man's secret region and his noblest part' – which he claims to have been 'privy to', and affirms that 'this inward place' was 'holy ground' where 'peace, and love, and grace / Kept house'. Secure in the belief that his friend encountered death in 'this safe state' and has been ushered into 'bliss', he abandons the lonely grief of the poem's introduction and tells him that he refuses 'to weep because thy course is run'. He is content to wait for the 'next glad news' of 'the Trumpet's summons from the dust'; and at the end, in a move that belongs more to the private than the public type of elegy, he looks to a future resurrection in which he will himself participate: 'Some bid their dead *good night!* but I will say / *Good morrow to dear Charles!* for it is day.'[7]

---

7 'To the Pious Memory of C.W. Esquire who Finished His Course Here, and Made His Entrance into Immortality upon the 13 of September, in the Year of Redemption 1653', *Complete Poems*, pp. 331-3.

III

It is in personal elegies like Ben Jonson's 'On My First Son' that the intricacies of the mourning process are explored with more sustained subjectivity – from the cry of desolation and bewilderment ('O, could I lose all father, now. For why / Will man lament the state he should envy?') to the painful acknowledgement that the seven years' lease granted by God on his 'loved boy' has come to its end 'on the just day' and the chastened vow with which he faces the future in the final line, 'As what he loves may never like too much'.[8] Similarly, the bereft husband of 'The Exequy' probes his own state of mind and the irrevocable nature of his loss – 'I Languish out, not Live the Day'; 'I find out / How lazily Time creepes about / To one that mournes'; 'Thy Sett / This Eve of blacknes did begett'; 'My last Good-night! Thou wilt not wake / Till I Thy Fate shall overtake' – and slowly resigns himself to 'wait my dissolution / With Hope and Comfort', sustained by the Christian belief that the day will come when 'wee shall Meet and Never part'.[9] Such poems bear out Dennis Kay's observation that the English elegy – 'every bit as much as the sonnet' in the period from Spenser to Milton – 'constituted a space in which writers felt encouraged to write introspectively, to make themselves their own subject'.[10]

In the work of Henry Vaughan, the experience of being an 'obscure mourner that would weep alone' is embodied most intensely in a series of untitled elegies in the 1650 *Silex Scintillans*. They were occasioned by the death of his younger brother, William, who died on or just before 14 July 1648, almost certainly as a consequence of his participation in the royalist rising in South Wales that led to a crushing defeat at the Battle of St Fagan's on 8 May.[11] From the placing of the elegies in the 1650 *Silex Scintillans* and time references within the texts, James Simmonds has calculated that the first four were composed during the seven weeks following William's death and another a year later in July 1649.[12] Two more were included among the new poems added to the second edition of

---

8 *Ben Jonson: The Complete Poems*, ed. George Parfitt (Harmondsworth: Penguin Books, 1975), p. 48.

9 *Poems of Henry King*, pp. 68-72.

10 Dennis Kay, *Melodious Tears: The English Funeral Elegy from Spenser to Milton* (Oxford: Clarendon Press, 1990), pp. 7-8.

11 For details of his death, see F.E. Hutchinson's *Henry Vaughan: A Life and Interpretation* (Oxford: Clarendon Press, 1947), pp. 95-7.

12 James D. Simmonds, 'The Date of Henry Vaughan's "Silex Scintillans"', *Notes and Queries* 205 (1960), 64-5. Another untitled poem, closely associated with the fourth in theme, may also be part of the series published in 1650.

Silex Scintillans in 1655.[13] The trauma of loss not only drove Vaughan inwards to contemplate his own sense of desolation but also led him to interpret the traumatic event in light of the deepening spiritual awareness that altered the direction of his life in the course of 1648.[14]

The first elegy, presumably written as the initial wave of grief overwhelmed him, is addressed to God in an effort to resist the common tendency to attribute the apparent injustice of an early death to some malignant or indifferent outside force:

> Thou that know'st for whom I mourn,
> And why these tears appear,
> That keep'st account, till he return
> Of all his dust left here;
> As easily thou might'st prevent
> As now produce these tears,
> And add unto that day he went
> A fair supply of years.[15]

This acknowledgement that the life-span of an individual is allotted by the deity fulfils the same function as the angry or accusatory questions found in many elegies – and, indeed, implies the question, 'Why did you elect to produce rather than prevent my tears of grief?'[16] In his Freudian analysis of elegiac conventions as 'literary versions of social and psychological practices' that make up 'a healthy work of mourning', Sacks observes that 'such questions actually carry that anger away from its possible attachment to the self' and adds that they also serve to 'deflect the closely related element' of guilt, which 'if unalleviated' would drag the mourner 'toward melancholy'.[17] Having stifled the questions that arise naturally in the first shock of bereavement, Vaughan makes the dangerous move into self-blame by relating the cause of his brother's death to the spiritual upheaval that is transforming his perspective upon the world:

---

13 There is a further elegy in the 1655 volume that is taken to be about Vaughan's first wife, who died in the early 1650s. For critical discussions of the elegies as a group, see A.J. Smith, 'Henry Vaughan's Ceremony of Innocence', *Essays and Studies* n.s. 26 (1973), 35-52; Stevie Davies, *Henry Vaughan* (Bridgend: Seren, Poetry of Wales Press, 1995), pp. 82-93; Rudrum, 'Henry Vaughan's Poems of Mourning'; and Naomi Marklew, '*Silex Scintillans*: Henry Vaughan's Interregnum Elegy', *Scintilla* No. 17 (2013), 36-51.

14 Vaughan's development into the religious poet of *Silex Scintillans* is discussed by E.L. Marilla, 'The Religious Conversion of Henry Vaughan', *Review of English Studies* 21 (1945), 15-22 and Hutchinson, *Life and Interpretation*, pp. 99-108.

15 *Complete Poems*, p. 170.

16 Compare Jonson's acceptance that the 'seven years' lease' on his son has been called in 'on the just day'.

17 Sacks, *The English Elegy*, pp. 2, 6, 22.

But 'twas my sin that forced thy hand
To cull this *prim-rose* out,
That by thy early choice forewarned
My soul might look about.

A reverie on the vanity and frailty of the human species concludes that 'Salvation' can only be attained through the 'painful throes' of 'Affliction', and this prompts a desire to 'know' his own 'end' and 'be as glad to find it' as his brother was. The poem does not conclude with a healthy reintegration into everyday life, which is the objective of Freud's 'work of mourning' – like Jonson's vow or King's 'Hope and Comfort' or Milton's 'Tomorrow to fresh woods, and pastures new'[18] – but with a prayer that he might soon emulate William in being fit to exchange this world for the heavenly kingdom:

Then make my soul white as his own,
My faith as pure, and steady,
And deck me, Lord, with the same crown
Thou hast crowned him already!

This poem and its conclusion illustrate Rudrum's remark that the subjects of the elegies in *Silex Scintillans* 'are praised either by implication, in the intensity of the sorrow and love expressed, or in terms that apply to all those who have been promoted from the Church Militant to the Church Triumphant'.[19]

As Naomi Marklew points out, the next elegy in the series – just three poems further on – omits the conventions of praise and consolation entirely, as the poet sinks into the unhealthy state of melancholia that Freud associated with the 'death-wish',[20] which is the negative corollary of the longing for heaven:

Come, come, what do I here?
Since he is gone
Each day is grown a dozen year,
And each hour, one;
Come, come!
Cut off the sum,
By these soiled tears!

---

18 'Lycidas', *John Milton: Complete Shorter Poems*, ed. John Carey, 2nd ed. (Harlow: Pearson/ Longman, 2007), p. 256.

19 Rudrum, 'Henry Vaughan's Poems of Mourning', p. 315.

20 Marklew, 'Henry Vaughan's Interregnum Elegy', pp. 43, 46.

King went through a similar phase of computing 'the weary howres' of mourning, but the belief that he would 'at last sitt downe' by his beloved saved him from the helpless sense of shame that alienates Vaughan here from both his God and his art:

> Strike these lips dumb:
> This restless breath
> That soils thy name,
> Will ne'er be tame
> Until in death.

The hopelessness that the death of William had precipitated in the poet's psyche did not rob him of his religious faith in an ultimate resurrection in the presence of God, but it seems to have intensified the inner turmoil caused by religious conversion and political catastrophe to plunge him in his darkest moments into a deep despair at the prospect of continuing existence in this life:

> Come, come!
> Such thoughts benumb;
> But I would be
> With him I weep
> A bed, and sleep
> To wake in thee.[21]

The next response to William's death has been called 'not an elegy but a thanksgiving'.[22] Its sudden move away from the life-denying melancholy of the previous poem – only a few pages before – should be seen as a necessary but not conclusive step in the elegiac project of coming to terms with bereavement. The joyful exclamations assert that a positive relationship is 'still' possible with the dead:

> Joy of my life! while left me here,
>   And still my love!
> How in thy absence thou dost steer
>   Me from above!
>   A life well led
>   This truth commends,
>   With quick, or dead
>   It never ends.

---

21 *Complete Poems*, pp. 173-4.
22 Davies, *Henry Vaughan*, p. 91.

The psychological function of elegy, after all, is to enact 'the process of discovery by which we who are the living learn what our significant dead mean to us'.[23] There is consolation in the 'truth' that the influence of a 'life well led' continues after death, even though it is equally true that 'the night / Is dark, and long' and that those who continue their pilgrimage in this world 'must pass / O'er dark hills, swift streams, and steep ways'. But the thought that 'God's saints are shining lights', shedding their beneficent 'beams' upon the pilgrims 'all night' and guiding them 'into bed' – the destination so longed for in the preceding elegy – brings an assurance that the grave is not the end of the journey, for the individual mourner or for the entire people of God:

> They are (indeed,) our pillar-fires
> Seen as we go,
> They are that City's shining spires
> We travel to;
> A swordlike gleam
> Kept man for sin
> First *out*; this beam
> Will guide him *in*.[24]

The biblical imagery of this final stanza – encompassing the expulsion of Adam and Eve from Paradise, the pillar of fire that led the Israelites to the promised land, and the heavenly city of the Book of Revelation – implies that the premature loss of William Vaughan has led his brother towards a deeper insight into the divine plan for history, in which the pain of individual loss can be sublimated in the vision of an eternal community bound together by a love that cannot be severed by death.

The long and dark 'night' of grieving is not so easy to escape from, however, and within four poems Vaughan is measuring out (as King had done) the creeping pace of time 'to one that mournes':

> Silence, and stealth of days! 'tis now
> Since thou art gone,
> Twelve hundred hours, and not a brow
> But clouds hang on.

Not yet reconciled to the irrecoverable loss of the earthly William, he reaches back to the moment when the light that animated his brother's body was extinguished:

23 Rudrum, 'Vaughan's Poems of Mourning', p. 317.
24 *Complete Poems*, pp. 177-8.

> So o'er fled minutes I retreat
> Unto that hour
> Which showed thee last, but did defeat
> Thy light, and power.

The effort to revive the living man in memory – 'I search, and rack my soul to see / Those beams again' – gives way to the brutal fact of the lifeless corpse, 'That dark, and dead sleeps in its known, / And common urn'. The poem enacts a grudging acceptance that here on earth he is left with only 'the snuff' of the candle that once burned brightly, so that 'now the spirit, not the dust / Must be thy brother.' This surrender of the earthly part of William to the 'common urn' of the grave is a crucial stage in the process of mourning. It brings with it the conviction that the one gift that can sustain him, while he himself remains 'in the heart of earth, and night', is the '*pearl*' of the Gospel, by the 'light' of which he will be able to 'Find Heaven, and thee'.[25]

In 'Sure, there's a tie of bodies!' – taken by Davies to be another in the series of elegies for William – the hermetic concept of a natural sympathy linking individual souls through the medium of the universal world-soul is extended by Vaughan to suggest that a similar sympathy exists between bodies. The flaw in this analogy, which offers momentary hope and solace, is quickly acknowledged by the poet himself:

> Sure, there's a tie of bodies! and as they
> Dissolve (with it,) to clay,
> Love languisheth, and memory doth rust
> O'er-cast with that cold dust.

As Davies interprets this, the 'energy which once flowed out from the dead person to the survivor' is cut off when the body dies, causing memories to 'degrade' and locking the speaker into 'a double-bind which sooner or later afflicts all who mourn'. The breaking of the link is nature's way of helping the 'hearts' of the bereaved to re-engage with the world, but the poet finds himself trapped into regarding 'this self-therapy' as 'a kind of apostasy', an act of 'infidelity' which leads the mind to 'affirm solidarity with the dead by denying community with the living'.[26] Hence the determination expressed in the final quatrain:

---

25 *Complete Poems*, pp. 180-1.

26 Davies, *Henry Vaughan*, pp. 86-90. Other discussions of the elegies omit this poem from the series, but it follows on from the point in the 'work of mourning' reached in 'Silence, and stealth of days!'

> But I will be mine own *death's-head*; and though
> The flatterer say, *I live*,
> Because incertainties we cannot know
> Be sure, not to believe.[27]

Resisting the invitation to live as if it were a temptation of the devil, the mourner once again chooses death.

The last of the elegies published in 1650, beginning 'I walked the other day (to spend my hour) / Into a field', narrates in semi-allegorical terms an experience that took place when 'winter' had 'ruffled all the bower' in which the speaker had 'digged about' to find the root of a 'gallant flower' that once bloomed there. The concluding lines – 'At whose dumb urn / Thus all the year I mourn' – and its position almost at the end of the volume, however, appear to date its composition to the anniversary of his brother's death in July 1649. It records the poet's comforting discovery that burial is part of a natural and providential cycle of regeneration, in which the body, like a plant, lives on 'fresh and green' underground until it is time to come forth 'most fair and young'. This prompts a prayer that the speaker may spend the rest of his life following the 'sacred way' that leads upwards to the place where 'light, joy, leisure, and true comforts move / Without all pain'; but, as Davies observes, the positive lesson communicated in this 'testimony of experience' does not prevent the renewed pain of plumbing once more 'the depths of his own psyche, with their buried mental contents' and 'recapitulating William's death-scene' in the poem's middle stanza:[28]

> This passed, I threw the clothes quite o'er his head,
> And stung with fear
> Of my own frailty dropped down many a tear
> Upon his bed.[29]

The ambivalence of 'bed' also allows the fantasy of digging up the root of a flower to be read as a suppressed yearning to recover his brother's body from the grave.

The third of the new poems published in the 1655 edition of *Silex Scintillans*, developing the earlier image of the holy dead as 'shining lights', ascribes a

---

27 *Complete Poems*, p. 185.
28 Davies, *Henry Vaughan*, p. 112.
29 *Complete Poems*, pp. 240-2.

positive role to memory as it charts another step towards recovery from the darkness of loss:

> They are all gone into the world of light!
> And I alone sit ling'ring here;
> Their very memory is fair and bright,
> And my sad thoughts doth clear.[30]

Further on in the volume, an elegy for his first wife pays tribute to the part she played in his rehabilitation – 'Fair and young light! my guide to holy / Grief and soul-curing melancholy' – and one more elegy for William pays a final poetic visit to the 'humble grave / Set with green herbs, glad hopes and brave', in which his brother 'lies / In death's dark mysteries' until the natural and spiritual dimensions of his being are reunited in resurrection: 'For whose dry dust green branches bud / And robes are bleached in the *Lamb*'s blood.'[31]

Stevie Davies's phrase 'anatomy of grief' implies something too deliberate and forensic for what the reader encounters in the elegies generated by the death of William Vaughan; her other phrase, 'self-therapy', is nearer the mark; but perhaps even more accurate is A.J. Smith's formulation: 'it is itself active experience, an engagement of the whole consciousness'.[32] One might add that the complete series constitutes a poetic rendering of the psychological and spiritual dimensions of 'the work of mourning' that is unequalled in the early modern era.[33] Noting that 'the lines between private and public losses were increasingly blurred' during the political turmoil of the mid-century, Naomi Marklew argues that the formal elegies do not only enact Vaughan's private grief for William but also play their part in the 'extended elegiac meditation for the loss of his king and Royalist cause' that is embodied in the 1655 *Silex Scintillans* 'in its entirety'.[34] Such a blurring of lines was in Vaughan's mind when he composed the preface to that volume in September 1654, offering it to 'the *Church*' in the hope that it might be 'as useful now in the *public*, as it hath been to me in *private*'.[35]

---

30 *Complete Poems*, pp. 246-7.

31 *Complete Poems*, pp. 279-80, 278-9. For a discussion of the elegy on Catherine Vaughan, see Rudrum, 'Vaughan's Poems of Mourning', pp. 319-25; and for a detailed analysis of 'As time one day by me did pass', see Smith, 'Vaughan's Ceremony of Innocence', 38-48.

32 Davies, *Henry Vaughan* pp. 85, 89; Smith, 'Vaughan's Ceremony of Innocence', 52.

33 Tennyson's *In Memoriam* contains a similarly comprehensive treatment of the effect of a deeply personal loss on an individual mind and sensibility.

34 Marklew, 'Vaughan's Interregnum Elegy', 36.

35 *Complete Poems*, p. 142.

IV

Vaughan wrote one other formal elegy, 'Daphnis. An Elegiac Eclogue', which has been largely neglected or misunderstood. It was not published until 1678 in *Thalia Rediviva*, and its date, its subject, and its integrity as a work of art have all been open to question because of six lines that clearly refer to the death and burial of the poet's twin brother in 1666.[36] For Vaughan's first modern editor, the poem was unequivocally 'on the death of the Rev'd Thomas Vaughan'.[37] Most subsequent commentators, however, have accepted Hutchinson's theory that it was written much earlier to commemorate a younger man (possibly William Vaughan) and then clumsily adapted, perhaps to provide a transition between Henry's work and the posthumous collection of his twin brother's Latin verses in the latter part the 1678 volume. In support of his argument, Hutchinson cited certain 'expressions' that chimed with 'Henry Vaughan's view of public events in the late forties, but would ill fit the years in which his brother Thomas was happily employed in the service of the restored king'.[38] Indeed, there is much to suggest that the death which originally prompted this elegy was of far greater public significance in the world of the late 1640s than the loss of a brother or a wife. In the first place, the neo-classical form of pastoral elegy had been developed during the Renaissance as a vehicle for allegory, often of a political kind, and Milton's 'Lycidas' in particular – Vaughan's principal contemporary model – was a 'polemically intended reformist poem' that 'seems to ask the reader to become partisan'.[39] And in the second place, Virgil's Fifth Eclogue – which provided the name Daphnis as well as material for several passages in Vaughan's text – was interpreted in the widely-read ancient

36 *Thalia Rediviva* was a late volume containing many poems that had not found a place in Vaughan's other published works. Thomas's burial by Sir Robert Moray near Oxford is referred to in lines 113-18.

37 See *Silex Scintillans: Sacred Poems and Private Ejaculations by Henry Vaughan*, ed. H.F. Lyte (London: Pickering, 1847), p. 224.

38 Hutchinson, *Life and Interpretation*, pp. 220-1. He acknowledges a debt to Louise Guiney in offering this solution to the problems posed by 'Daphnis'. For the alternative case that it is one of Vaughan's 'few indisputably Restoration poems', written 'entirely in 1666 for the death of his twin brother', see Cedric C. Brown, 'The Death of Righteous Men: Prophetic Gesture in Vaughan's "Daphnis" and Milton's *Lycidas*', *George Herbert Journal*, 7 (1983/4), 1-24 and Graeme J. Watson, 'Political Change and Continuity of Vision in Henry Vaughan's "Daphnis. An Elegiac Eclogue"', *Studies in Philology* 83 (1986), 158-81.

39 Cedric C. Brown, *John Milton's Aristocratic Entertainments* (Cambridge: Cambridge University Press, 1985), pp. 158, 164. 'Lycidas' was initially printed in the memorial volume, *Justa Eduardo King Naufrago* (1638), and then reprinted in Milton's *Poems* (1645) with a headnote claiming that it had foretold 'the ruin of our corrupted clergy then in their height' (*Complete Shorter Poems*, p. 243). Hutchinson thought the 'echoes' of Milton's text in 'Daphnis' were 'more likely to have originated at an earlier date than 1666' (*Life and Interpretation*, p. 221).

commentary by Servius as an elegy on the death of the great general and statesman Julius Caesar.[40] The question with which Vaughan's poem opens – 'What clouds, *Menalcas*, do oppress thy brow?' – is reminiscent of a phrase near the beginning of one of the elegies for William Vaughan – 'and not a brow / But clouds hang on'; but this elegy is a conversation between two shepherds sharing their grief and despair rather than the subjective monologue of a mourner who 'would weep alone'. The oppressive clouds are attributed initially to the loss of an idyllic pastoral scene – 'The green wood glittered with the golden sun / And all the west like silver shined' – which was destroyed by 'fierce dark showers' and 'lightenings' that 'burned' the air. Only then, by way of a simile, is this associated with the death of an individual: 'And *Daphnis* so, just so is *Daphnis* dead!' Read allegorically in the context of the period that produced Vaughan's personal elegies on his younger brother, this sounds like a poetic evocation of the way civil war erupted into the peaceful Caroline world and culminated in the execution of Charles I, another Daphnis to set beside the assassinated Julius Caesar.

It is not part of my purpose to rehearse again the evidence for a claim I have made elsewhere that 'Daphnis' is Vaughan's great formal elegy on the dead king.[41] What interests me here is the skill with which Vaughan has adapted the genre of pastoral elegy to capture the experience of a particular community at a precise historical moment.[42] In his hands, it can evoke the golden age of boyhood in the Usk valley under the 'goodly shelter' of an oak tree that was both a feature of Matthew Herbert's rectory garden at Llangattock, where he and Thomas were taught their love of poetry by 'old *Amphion*', and a symbol of the peaceful phase of Charles I's reign during which the arts had flourished; and it can share a moment of hope for better times with fellow royalists 'when but one twinkling star / Peeps betwixt clouds, more black than is our tar'. But it can also pour vengeful scorn upon those who 'madly hate, and persecute the

---

40 See D.L. Drew, 'Virgil's Fifth Eclogue: A Defence of the Julius Caesar-Daphnis Theory', *The Classical Quarterly* 16 (1922), 57-64.

41 Suffice it to note that the description of Daphnis as 'the brave sufferer' recalls the subtitle of the *Eikon Basilike* — *The Portraicture of His Sacred Majestie in His Solitudes and Sufferings*; that the image of 'worth oppressed' which 'palm-like bravely overtops the weight' was displayed graphically in the famous frontispiece and that the phrase 'feral birds' occurs in the text of the same book; and that the vow to 'yearly keep the holyday of swains' in 'solemn honour' of Daphnis was observed for many years by royalists on the anniversary of Charles I's execution. The case is set out in more detail in my '"Daphnis. An Elegiac Eclogue" by Henry Vaughan', *Durham University Journal* n.s. 36 (1974), 25-40; and *The Writing of Royalism 1628-1660* (Cambridge: Cambridge University Press, 2001), pp. 299-306.

42 Kay describes pastoral elegy as a form in which 'from ancient times . . . consciousness of tradition, repetition, translation, and imitation was inseparable from innovation and invention' (*Melodious Tears*, p. 4).

light'; and it can counteract with 'fair truth' such works as *Eikonoklastes*, in which 'false, foul prose-men' like Milton had denigrated the dead king. The prevailing mood, however, is one of 'fatal sadness', in which 'Heaven's just displeasure & our unjust ways' have brought 'plagues, dearth and decays' upon 'our lands', where 'feral birds send forth unpleasant notes' and 'night (the nurse of thoughts,) sad thoughts promotes'.[43] In this elegy, Jonathan Post complains, 'grief is not effectively purged' and nature is not 'restored to a more innocent, beneficent, and fruitful state'.[44] But in the months following the beheading of the king in January 1649, Vaughan's perspective on the political situation in Breconshire and further afield was stuck at the stage of mourning he had expressed with such devastating honesty in the first two elegies on the death of William – racked with guilt and sunk so deeply in despair that any alleviation in this world seemed impossible. As an elegy, 'Daphnis' may have failed to complete the expected journey towards psychic rehabilitation, but there is both courage and artistic integrity in the way it articulates the traumatized condition of the royalist remnant in its darkest hour.

43 The quotations from 'Daphnis' are from *Complete Poems*, pp. 385-90.
44 Jonathan Post, *Henry Vaughan: The Unfolding Vision* (Princeton, N.J.: Princeton University Press, 1982), p. 231.

'Bridge Llangattock over the Monmouthshire Canal'
by Christopher Werrett

MARIA APICHELLA

David Calls

> I'm ignoring him   No,
> I'm answering   leaving this shaded cloister.

I throw open the doors. David's camping beyond
the boundaries, teasing on the horizon's
edge.

'Don't
be afraid of the dark,' he says.
'Where you are going I have gone.'

The night is present. It rubs
against me like a cat.
Drizzle, little slaps of wind. The stars spit
on this steep slip-shod road. How long
have I edged through pockets of closed fields?
Past silhouettes of cautious sheep.

I fear the groan
of mother-cows – the shock
of sudden crows, rising.
A mosquito worries close,
bites of doubt appear.
So much could go wrong with the moon
on the move, these dark sky tricks
the sudden curve of cliffs and
should I be here?

I am on the way. Galumphing
towards my Love in walking boots,
smelling like puddles, salt. The night
smeared across my face.

Hitch me
to him like a caravan to a bumper.
I am coming
stupidly as the stars are of mighty use.

Deuteronomy Reads

If with your throat,
fingers,
bowels,
you choose to follow fully, blessings
will sprout
like Queen Anne's lace; escort you as scent;
blackberries, Welsh rain,
stone. You'll be blessed in Aberystwyth,
in the bathroom.
The lyrics on your screen, the extension of your mind,
every page of every hardback you skim
– all your friends, your flat pack desk, keys,
green lamp will be hallowed
when you sleep, rise, and on
it goes.

If with your throat,
fingers,
bowels,
you choose to play
games with Yahweh, cherry-
picking principles, curses
like athlete's foot will spread from your soles.
You will be tormented in Aberystwyth,
in the bathroom. The language
on your screen,
the procedure of your mind, every page of every book
you absorb – all your people, your desk, keys,
your green lamp will be troubled.
You will be cursed when you start,
when you finish.

David cocks his eyebrow.
'So primitive.'

Bless me,

please. Curses
are little weights and I'm heavy enough.

Tip blessings on me when I'm outside.
Throw them at me when I arrive
at the door. Slip them in my tea
when we meet. Stir them into my words.

Dunk me in pools of blessing, stuff me
like olives. Rub them into the skin
of my hands. Multiply within my life
like cells in my bones. Let them rise
before me like fog, grow under my feet,

shoot back at me when I sneeze.

MATTHEW BARTON

Burial Chamber

Ronas Hill, Shetland

Not just a cairn at the top but a chamber,
a mouth eating light I found after the clamber

up screeside to the top with the lurch of a pure
shelve-off to seascape and skyscape, rare deepening blue

and me at the centre as always of all that far
fold-out of distance, stuck in one point of view

like the fly in the ointment, the hole in a tooth
the tongue of the world keeps touching. I was loth

to enter the chamber but somehow that was the answer
to a question I hadn't yet asked. Open it there

stood dark and oracular, muttering its truth
so I bent down, crawled into the fear

of my life, earth's dank lap
and lay on my back looking up

at the lid of stone locked
close over my face, and no more to be said.

Except what had been a black gap
in the world from outside inside was fractured with light

and I started to breathe like a baby, a soul in its swaddle
of rib and flesh. Wind sang like a kettle

one moment, next whumped like a heart
as if wombed here I heard

the pulse of a mother;
and all said and done

death suddenly seemed like another
way to be born.

31

Backwoods

A stand of pines
a needle-strewn
silence ringed in fern.

Sun flashlights the scene.
It takes a moment to take in
the actions of my kind:

every tree has been
lacerated. One
stripped to white bone.

Scores and slashes – trunks
gashed to the quick. Birds sing
light shines

on a tangle of chain,
snapped blades, crushed cans.
Was it just wanton

rage or were they cleansed
by these rites – scars written
here for earth to mend?

It mends or tries to, patiently it mends:
resin thickens from the wounds
I dip a finger in, smear unguent

on my skin.

Balancing Act

For Philippe Petit (New York 1974)

The moment before
he steps on the crying wire
who knows if he'll fall?
It spools from him, strings
his guts on the wind. The siren ground
sings up. But at the edge he frees
his feet from everything holding him,
becomes

his mast, sails off

so far already beyond the small
saving of his skin.
It's then
they see the smile rise through him, know
he will not fall: is raised on nothing
less than all burden lifted, body
walking true its risen wave.

Reimagining Scriptural Places in the Writing of Henry Vaughan

JOSEPH ASHMORE

I

The imaginative reconstruction of scriptural scenes held an important position in early modern biblical hermeneutics. Readers were encouraged to recreate scriptural locations in their mind's eye and imagine themselves within biblical scenes. Demonstrating the effects of the figure *evidentia* ('vividness') in the Bible, Matthias Flacius Illyricus, one of the most influential Protestant scriptural commentators of the Renaissance, describes how a style of writing 'which sets out the matter to be inspected as if it were before the eyes [*sermo, qui res quasi ante oculos spectandas proponit*]' is one which

> does not only move the spirit [of the reader], but also joyously illustrates the very things which are to be seen and considered, while making them, so to speak, present; it thus brings about, as it were, a certain intuitive cognition (as the Scholastics term it)[.] . . . The holy Scriptures assuredly surpass many other texts in this mode of writing.[1]

Flacius blends together late-medieval metaphysics and classical rhetoric. The invocation of a Scholastic 'intuitive cognition' alludes to the epistemological process by which we come to know the 'contingent truth' of a situation, and which at-

---

1 Matthias Flacius Illyricus, *Clauis Scripturae Sacrae, seu de Sermone Sacrarum literarum*, 2 vols (Basle: Iohannes Oporinus & Eusebius Episcopius (vol. i), Paulus Quecus (vol. ii), 1567), ii, 359: 'Neque tamen talis sermo solum animum mouet, sed etiam res ipsas feliciter illustrat, dum eas ueluti coram spectandas contemplandasque proponit, atque ita ueluti intuitiuam quandam noticiam (ut scholae loquuntur) efficit . . . Sane sacrae Literae in hoc genere multos alios scriptores superant[.]' I have silently expanded contractions and lowered letters in quotations. Unless otherwise indicated, all translations are my own. Scriptural references are to *The Bible: Authorized King James Version*, with an introduction and notes by Robert Carroll and Stephen Pickett (Oxford: Oxford University Press, 1997). My thanks to Katrin Ettenhuber for all her help with this article.

tained its most influential form in the writing of William of Ockham.[2] Having quoted Horace's *Ars Poetica* immediately before this passage, Flacius places this model of cognition within the principles of classical rhetoric: *docere* ('*noticiam*'), *delectare* ('*feliciter*') and *movere* ('*animum mouet*').[3] The Bible provides a supreme example of a text's rhetorical ability to stimulate the reader's visual imagination, an instrumental process in the apprehension of scriptural truths. Flacius also implicitly theorises the reader's response: making a scriptural scene present to the mind's eye is both educative and affectively moving.[4] He is, however, hesitant about the mechanics of this process: his description of a text's capacity for imaginative visual immediacy is off-set by representational misgivings ('so to speak', 'as it were'). The idea of the mind's eye in early modern religious discourse was fraught with problematic questions which, perhaps, lie behind Flacius's verbal shifting. Idols could be set up as much in the mind as on the Rood screen.[5]

This article starts by examining the methods of reimagining scriptural locations set out by Flacius and adopted by Protestant readers and writers. Flacius enjoyed an enduring popularity until at least the end of the seventeenth century;[6]

---

2 See Ockham's *Ordinatio*: 'Et universaliter omnis notitia incomplexa termini vel terminorum, seu rei vel rerum, virtute cuius potest evidenter cognosci aliqua veritas contingens, maxime de praesenti, est notitia intuitiva' ['Intuitive cognition is, universally, all incomplex cognition of a term, or terms, or of a thing, or things, by the virtue of which any contingent truth can be clearly known, especially when it comes to matters in sight'], in William of Ockham, *Opera Philosophica et Theologica ad Fidem Codicum Manuscriptorum Edita: Opera Theologica*, 10 vols (St Bonaventure, NY: St Bonaventure University, 1967-86), I: *Scriptum in Librum Primum Sententiarum, Ordinatio: Prologus et Distinctio Prima*, ed. by Gedeon Gál and Stephen Brown (1967), pp. 31-32 (Liber I, Prol., Q.1). The Latin is quoted in John F. Boler, 'Intuitive and abstractive cognition', in *The Cambridge History of Later Medieval Philosophy: From the Rediscovery of Aristotle to the Disintegration of Scholasticism, 1100-1600*, ed. by Norman Kretzmann, Anthony Kenny and Jan Pinborg (Cambridge: Cambridge University Press, 1982), pp. 460-78 (p. 467, n. 37).

3 On the triadic rhetorical model, see e.g. *Sidney's 'The Defence of Poesy' and Selected Renaissance Literary Criticism*, ed. with an introduction and notes by Gavin Alexander (London: Penguin, 2004), p. xxxv, quoting Cicero, *De optimo genere oratorum*, 3: 'the best orator is the one who by his oratory instructs, pleases, and moves the minds of his audience.' Flacius's quotation of Horace (II, 359) is from *Ars Poetica*, ll. 180-82.

4 On *evidentia* (also known as *enargeia*) as the 'rhetoric of presence' in the Renaissance, see François Rigolot, 'The rhetoric of presence: art, literature, and illusion', in *The Cambridge History of Literary Criticism*, 9 vols (Cambridge: Cambridge University Press, 1989-2013), III: *The Renaissance*, ed. by Glyn P. Norton (1999), pp. 161-67.

5 For a useful survey of the mind's eye in the Renaissance, see Sarah Howe, *Literature and the Visual Imagination in Renaissance England, 1580-1620* (unpublished doctoral thesis, University of Cambridge, 2011), pp. 13-20; for its idolatrous potential, see Howe, pp. 80-130, and Stuart Clark, *Vanities of the Eye: Vision in Early Modern European Culture* (Oxford: Oxford University Press, 2007), pp. 167-72.

6 See Debora K. Shuger, *Sacred Rhetoric: The Christian Grand Style in the English Renaissance* (Princeton, NJ: Princeton University Press, 1988), pp. 71, 89, 115.

his interpretive strategies reflect a reading culture which valued the role of the visual imagination but sought to confine its idolatrous potential. The second half of my argument will look at the religious writing of Henry Vaughan in the light of the acts of visually imaginative reading which Flacius sets out. Vaughan places his speakers in the spatial environs of a scriptural passage, but he also engages with this hermeneutic strategy in chronological terms: placing oneself in a biblical scene is an act of time-travel as much as a shift in location. For Vaughan, however, these acts of spatial and historical recreation are problematic. Scripturally constructed locations reveal differences between the ways in which God communicated in the past and in Vaughan's own situation. Writing at a time of religious upheaval and liturgical privation, Vaughan places acute pressure on the process of finding God through acts of scriptural reading. The difficulties he finds in Flacius's hermeneutic method reflect a context in which biblical interpretation was placed under intense scrutiny.

I hope also to contest a strand of criticism which reads the visualisation of scriptural locations as indicative of a Catholic meditative tradition. To be sure, as Louis Martz has shown in his reading of seventeenth-century poets, the *compositio loci* was a key component of Counter-Reformation pre-meditation exercises.[7] In response to Martz's suggestion of Catholic influence, Barbara Lewalski has suggested that 'Protestant meditation did not stimulate the senses to recreate and imagine biblical scenes in vivid detail; it would not therefore give rise to poetry based upon visual imagery and sensuous immediacy'.[8] I suggest, however, that Lewalski overstates the rejection of recreated 'biblical scenes' – 'visual imagery' is not always concomitant with 'sensuous immediacy'.[9] Furthermore, we can find precedents for reimagining scriptural locations outside of a meditative tradition. By attending to the specific spatial and textual circumstances of a scriptural scene, Protestant writers attempted to situate timelessly significant events (for instance, the Crucifixion or the Ascension) in historical and geographical actuality. Readers directed their mind's eye to scriptural places (rather than, say, Christ on the cross) in order to evade imaginative idolatry.

---

7 Louis L. Martz, *The Poetry of Meditation: A Study in English Religious Literature of the Seventeenth Century*, rev. edn (New Haven, CT: Yale University Press, 1962); pp. 27-32 deal specifically with *compositio loci*.

8 Barbara Kiefer Lewalski, *Protestant Poetics and the Seventeenth-Century Religious Lyric* (Princeton, NJ: Princeton University Press, 1979), p. 150.

9 See Michael Bath, *Speaking Pictures: English Emblem Books and Renaissance Culture* (Harlow: Longman, 1994), pp. 218-19, for an analogous response to Lewalski's argument in the context of emblematics.

II

In the section of the *Clauis* dealing with *evidentia*, Flacius presents scripture as an unsurpassed storehouse of rhetorical examples. As mentioned, he also outlines models for reading the scriptures:

> [The figure *evidentia*] places the matter before our eyes as an even fuller exposition of the subject, all with the end that its various circumstances are also carefully set forth: [that is,] when those things which precede and follow it are, moreover, considered at the same time, and also that which is itself to be understood; or when a part of the matter is more clearly unfolded, and, the meaning of the words having been revealed, is copiously illustrated and depicted[.] . . . Thus often in the gospels the place, time, people and occasions are indicated.[10]

A scriptural passage yields a large amount of material for an unmistakably visual imaginative process. The parts of the scriptural scene can be built up in two ways: the familiar Augustinian strategy of attending to textual context ('those things which precede and follow it') is complemented by copious 'illustrat[ion]' of the attributes of the scene itself.[11] Flacius's description of rhetorical effect, moreover, shifts the interpretive onus to the reader's own activity. In the space implied by the passive verbs is the figure of an industrious reader collating textual 'circumstances' – 'the place, time, people and occasions', as well as the surrounding scriptural passages – into an imaginative tableau of the scriptural text.

The motive behind Flacius's interpretive suggestions is found in his classical sources. Collating and picturing the circumstances of a situation was a fundamental technique in forensic oratory, through which the orator could make his auditors eyewitnesses to an event. For Quintilian, *enargeia* (another term for *evidentia*) is a way of expressing the matter 'clearly and in such a way that it seems to be actually seen'.[12] The figure is synonymic with *hypotyposis*, which includes

---

10 Flacius, II, 362: 'Duodecimo, ante oculos rem proponit etiam plenior rei expositio, cum causae omnes, item uariae circumstantiae eius accurate exponuntur: cum item antecedentia & sequentia simul recensentur, & ipsa quoque cognoscenda res, aut totius negocii pars clarius euoluitur, & apertis significantibusque uerbis copiose illustratur & depingitur, . . . Sic saepe in Euangelistis locus, tempus, personae & occasiones indicantur.' This is part of a numerated list of rhetorical effects, and the subject of 'proponit' etc. is ambiguous (I have taken it to be the figure *evidentia* itself).

11 See Augustine, *On Christian Teaching*, trans. by R.P.H. Green (Oxford: Oxford University Press, 1997), III.4 (p. 68). I refer to the book and marginal section numbers in Green's edition.

12 *Institutio Oratoria*, 8.3.62. All references (given parenthetically) are to the text and translation in Quintilian, *The Orator's Education*, ed. and trans. by Donald A. Russell, Loeb Classical Library, 5 vols (Cambridge, MA: Harvard University Press, 2001); here, vol. III, 374-75.

topographia, the '[c]lear and vivid descriptions of places' (9.2.44). This can be achieved through 'somehow paint[ing]' a scene 'in words' (8.3.63), through accumulating 'a number of details' (8.3.66), and by drawing attention to 'incidental features' (8.3.70). The emphasis on the visual clarity of the recreation of a scene in the 'mind's eye' (8.3.62) has interpretive implications for the auditors which recall Aristotle's preference for plausibility over possibility in the *Poetics*. Vivid descriptions apply to scenes which are 'plausible', even if some elements are invented (8.3.70), and show us '*how* [an event] took place' (9.2.40).

Flacius is clearly indebted to the classical forensic preference for imaginatively visualised matter.[13] By extension, this visualisation lends a sense of historical plausibility to the situation imagined and facilitates narrative comprehension. Unlike Quintilian, however, Flacius emphasises the reader's interpretive activity, and continuously directs him or her back to the scriptural text. Unlike the fictions constructed by Roman orators, moreover, scripture will, to Flacius's mind, always speak the truth to the reader. Flacius's case is reflected in contemporary rhetorical theory. Henry Peacham's *Garden of Eloquence* (1577 edition) similarly reinvents classical rhetoric for scriptural interpretation; without it, 'no man can reade profytably, or vnderstand perfectlye, eyther Poets, Oratours, or the holy Scriptures'.[14] He defines *hypotyposis* as 'a discription of persons, things, places, and tymes' which is effected 'by a diligent gathering togeather of circumstaunces'; the matter is expressed 'so plainely, that it seemeth rather paynted in tables, then expressed with wordes, and the hearer shall rather thincke he see it, then heare it'.[15]

How does a strategy for interpreting scripture which invokes 'paynted . . . tables' avoid idolatry? I want to suggest that the stress on establishing textual and historical context is an attempt to safeguard this interpretive method against the dangers of image-worship, not least because it appeals to historical plausibility and truthful representation, as opposed to man-made fictions. We have seen that Flacius invokes Ockhamist epistemology to secure the truth-value of imaginative recreation in a scriptural context. For Peacham, the description of a location, *topographia*, is the 'euident and true description of a place'.[16] Quintilian's link between plausibility and *evidentia* is transformed by Peacham into a truth-claim for imaginatively visible ('euident') description. *Topographia* is distinguished from *topothesia* ('when we descrybe a place, and yet no such place').[17] In the 1593 edition of *The Garden of Eloquence*, Peacham suggests

---

13 See Flacius, II, 359.
14 Henry Peacham, *The Garden of Eloquence: Conteyning the Figures of Grammer and Rhetorick* (London: H. Jackson, 1577), sig. A3r.
15 Peacham, *Garden* (1577), sig. O2r.
16 Peacham, *Garden* (1577), sig. P1r.
17 Peacham, *Garden* (1577), sig. P1v.

that *topothesia*, a figure of 'fained description', is 'proper to Poets, and is seldom vsed of Orators'; this discrimination is made precisely because Peacham's conception of *descriptio* in oratory is invested in conveying true circumstances.[18]

The emphasis on 'true description' is crucial in the re-imagination of scriptural places. An English translation of Christiaan van Adrichem's *Vrbis Hierosolimae quemadmodum ea Christi tempore floruit . . . breuis descriptio* (1585) exhorts the reader to use this 'liuely plot, or map' to envisage Christ's sufferings in the Passion 'euen as if they were now donne before our eies'.[19] This understanding of Christ's pains is constructed through topographical description rather than a depiction of the crucified Christ. The translator's preface applies Peacham's insistence on the truth of *topographia* to a confessional argument which hinges on an appeal to historical plausibility. The spatial circumstances aim at establishing a basis of historical truth:

> [B]icause the maister workeman [van Adrichem] in this new plat of ould decayed *Ierusalem*, hath left behind him sum rubbish and reliques of the Romish superstition, I haue in some measure purged and swept the stretes and corners of the same, with the broome of truth, and carying them out by the Scouregate haue layed them on the Leystall of obliuion.[20]

Tymme's 'broome of truth' has swept away anachronistic accruements which prevent our reconstruction of an accurately historicised Jerusalem ('rubbish') and distract our devotional attention ('reliques'). At the same time, he is also aware of the historical distance between CE 33 and 1595. The 'plat' is 'new' but the city 'decayed'. Despite this paradoxical presentation, the Protestant reader is able to subvert centuries of (allegedly) superstitious tradition, and ground the imaginative reconstruction of a biblical narrative in a historically verifiable landscape: the 'plat' provides the circumstances for understanding the 'plot' of Christ's Passion. While I can make no claims for the accuracy of van Adrichem's description, I do want to suggest that Tymme's argument is part of broader Protestant fiction which saw the recreation of the spatial contexts of scripture

---

18 *Henry Peachams "The Garden of Eloquence" (1593): Historisch-kritische Einleitung, Transkription und Kommentar*, ed. by Beate-Maria Koll, Literarische Studien 4 (Frankfurt am Main: Peter Lang, 1996), p. 139. As Koll explains, 'Auf gar keinen Fall aber ist Vortäuschen oder Verfälschen ein Kennzeichen der *Descriptio*. Die Figuren *Topothesia* und *Prosographia*, die auf dieser Basis angelegt sind, kommen für rhetorische Rede kaum oder gar nicht in Frage' (p. cii). ['Feigning or falsification is under no circumstances characteristic of *descriptio*. The figures of *topothesia* and *prosographia*, which are established on these grounds, rarely or never play a role in rhetorical oratory.']

19 Christiaan van Adrichem, *A Briefe Description of Hierusalem and of the Suburbs therof, as it florished in the time of Christ*, trans. by Thomas Tymme (London: Peter Short, 1595), sig. ¶4r.

20 van Adrichem, sig. ¶2v.

as not only following established interpretive strategies (Augustine, for instance, saw topographies as useful exegetical aids),[21] but as a means of sidestepping the idolatrous potential of the visual imagination when reading the Bible by appealing to a set of historically plausible circumstances, and returning geographically, as it were, *ad fontes*.

Reconstructing scriptural scenes in the mind's eye was an important strategy in Protestant exegesis. The moments when seventeenth-century writers place their speakers in biblical landscapes can be read in the light of the earlier context I have established. In particular, the religious writing of Henry Vaughan embodies a response to the models of circumstantial recreation that Flacius and others propose. Vaughan interrogates the imaginative leaps in time and space which these models require. How, he asks, is this interpretive strategy useful for working out one's relation to God across historical distance? How can Vaughan's historical circumstances be transcended?

III

Vaughan's writing is recognised for its rich scriptural texture. As Philip West has shown, Vaughan uses the Bible for a variety of purposes.[22] Scripture is, in Vaughan's words, 'lifes guide' for the Protestant reader at pragmatic, moral and soteriological levels.[23] One of his strategies for scriptural reference is the invocation of a specific biblical location – Eden, Jacob's Well, the Mount of Olives. Eluned Brown has shown that Vaughan's recreation of biblical landscapes serves a typological purpose, and attempts to find 'God-in-history'.[24] Lewalski is also correct in identifying Vaughan's typologically-informed use of a 'quasi-biblical landscape' in which he situates his pilgrim-like speakers.[25] I want, however, to revise these accounts of Vaughan's deployment of scriptural locations by examining the ways in which Vaughan's writing investigates the exegetical strategies which involve thinking oneself back in time to a biblical scene, and which resist typological models of interpretation.

---

21 Augustine, II.110.
22 Philip West, *Henry Vaughan's 'Silex Scintillans': Scripture Uses* (Oxford: Oxford University Press, 2001).
23 'To the Holy Bible' (*Silex Scintillans* (1655)), line 1. References to Vaughan's poetry, given parenthetically, will be to the text, titles and line numbers in *The Works of Henry Vaughan*, ed. by L.C. Martin, 2nd edn (Oxford: Clarendon Press, 1957).
24 Eluned Brown, 'Henry Vaughan's Biblical Landscape', *Essays and Studies*, n.s., 30 (1977), 50-60 (p. 55).
25 Lewalski, p. 328.

Allan and Helen Wilcox have drawn attention to Vaughan's 'profoundly meta-physical' conception of 'sacred space'.[26] They are right to suggest that Vaughan, at times, conceives of God as unrestricted by spatial limits. In 'The World' (*Silex Scintillans* (1650)), the speaker turns away from spatially restrictive 'grots, and caves' (51), and attempts to find 'The way which from this dead and dark abode / Leads up to God' (53-54). Nonetheless, Vaughan frequently practises a process of scriptural interpretation that attempts to trace God in the physical environs of a biblical scene. The Mount of Olives, for instance, constitutes a geographical location, still accessible through scripture and the reader's imagination, which bears witness to Christ's presence on earth. However, Vaughan also problematises the historical distance between biblical sites, and implicitly acknowledges that focusing on a particular textual and topographical place risks depriving us of our grasp on the whole scope of the Bible.

For Vaughan, the problems posed by reading and reimagining scriptural places are fundamentally epistemological. How can Christ's eternal salvific role, as well as his exemplary conduct, continue to be understood through ancient New Testament narratives when his bodily presence is no longer to be found upon earth? Recreating biblical scenes can only offer limited assistance when it comes to finding the Saviour who once inhabited them. At the same time, these epistemological limitations are inseparably related to Vaughan's historical and political situation. John N. Wall, focusing on *Silex* (1650) in particular, has drawn connections between the difficult processes of scriptural interpretation performed by Vaughan's poems and the proscription of Church of England liturgy from 1645.[27] Deprived of a community which offered interpretive guidance and sacramental ritual, Vaughan's readers are directed to recalibrate their interpretive and epistemological resources. 'The Search' (*Silex* (1650)), for instance, shows the vanity of the 'speaker's categories of expectation' that he might find Christ through his own 'powers of interpretation'.[28] Instead, Vaughan's readers are directed by the speaker's example to adopt an 'eschatological perspective', and frame interpretive failure – here, the inability to find Christ where he is expected to be found – within an attitude of 'expectant endurance' which defers to God's overarching soteriological plan.[29]

Wall's account is instructive because it draws out the epistemological implications of Vaughan's 'Anglican survivalism' when it comes to scriptural inter-

---

26 Allan and Helen Wilcox, 'Matter and Spirit Conjoined: Sacred Places in the Poetry of George Herbert, Henry Vaughan, R.S. Thomas and Rowan Williams', *Scintilla*, 11 (2007), 133-51 (p. 142).

27 John N. Wall, *Transformations of the Word: Spenser, Herbert, Vaughan* (Athens, GA: University of Georgia Press, 1988), pp. 273-365, and esp. pp. 301-41.

28 Wall, p. 323.

29 Wall, pp. 340, 339.

pretation, and also because it implies that, in the context of liturgical suppression, exegetical methods in private scriptural reading are placed under intense pressure.[30] I do want, however, to suggest that Wall's analysis depends too much on the liturgy and an 'identifying community' of Church of England worshippers for the arbitration of scriptural meaning and direction in biblical interpretation.[31] Vaughan did indeed associate closely with ministers deposed from their positions in 1650 (including his brother), and his local church was probably unused for an extended period in the Interregnum; his response to his Church's beleaguered historical position is undeniable.[32] Yet the methods of interpretation which Vaughan's examples of scriptural reading imply – above all, in this case, the scrutiny of scriptural scenes – can also be placed in relation to questions about scriptural semiotics and the specifically textual 'kind of mediation' and 'version of the truth' conveyed by the Bible which have a broader contextual significance.[33] That is to say, Vaughan's treatment of scriptural places bears witness both to an acute set of historical pressures that make finding and affirming Christ's presence problematic, and to an ongoing discourse about scriptural rhetoric, the relation between word and spirit and the role of the devotional imagination.

Vaughan's poetics constitutes in part an attempt to offer scriptural landscapes as a suitable subject for devotional poetry. 'Mount of Olives [I]' (*Silex* (1650)), a poem not often addressed by Vaughan's critics, reacts against a secular genre of landscape poetry, and attempts to channel the poetic attention away from potentially idolatrous subjects. The speaker should not 'allow / Language to love / And Idolize some shade, or grove' (2-4), or, indeed, other hills such as '*Cotswold*' or (in Denham's case) '*Coopers*' (9):

> such ill-plac'd wit,
> Conceit, or call it what you please
> Is the braines fit,
> And meere disease[.]
> (5-8)

---

30 On Vaughan's relation to 'Anglican survivalism' (a term coined by John Morrill), see Claude J. Summers, 'Herrick, Vaughan, and the Poetry of Anglican Survivalism', in *New Perspectives on the Seventeenth-Century English Religious Lyric*, ed. by John R. Roberts (Columbia, MO: University of Missouri Press, 1994), pp. 46-74.

31 Wall, p. 277.

32 See Wall, p. 278; Alan Rudrum, 'Resistance, Collaboration, and Silence: Henry Vaughan and Breconshire Royalism', in *The English Civil Wars in the Literary Imagination*, ed. by Claude J. Summers and Ted-Larry Pebworth (Columbia, MO: University of Missouri Press, 1999), pp. 102-118 (pp. 103-105); Robert Wilcher, *The Writing of Royalism: 1628-1660* (Cambridge: Cambridge University Press, 2001), p. 324.

33 West, p. 13.

Vaughan frames an argument for the potential vanity of poetic creation in specifically spatial terms. In 'Idle Verse' (*Silex* (1650)), his sinful 'queint folies' (1) are described with the same rhetoric of disease: they are 'Blind, desp'rate *fits*' (9), and 'The idle talk of feav'rish souls' (15). The humoral imbalance of physical sickness points towards an equivalent disequilibrium between poetic text and sacred subject; this is both a physical and a spiritual 'Blind[ness]'. In 'Mount of Olives [I]', however, this sickened 'wit' is literally 'ill-plac'd'. Alongside references to contemporary writing, Vaughan implicitly addresses an entire poetic tradition. Parnassus (The 'Poets . . . hill' (17-18)) and the Helicon (their 'fountaine' (19)) should be relocated in scripture. The 'learned swaines' (10) of Virgil's eclogues have no place here; the speaker states that the Mount has heard 'both reed / And sheepward play' (15-16), alluding to the Psalmist's 'cornet' (Psalm 98.6), and David and Christ as literal and figurative shepherds. Vaughan's Christianisation of a secular poetics invites us, at Alan Rudrum's suggestion, to compare 'Mount of Olives [I]' with Herbert's 'Jordan' poems.[34] Yet this comparison also highlights a salient difference between Herbert's and Vaughan's poetry. Herbert's Jordan serves as a symbol of baptism and renewal, but the poems do not feature any sort of geographical river. Vaughan's Mount, on the other hand, is the addressee of the speaker's apostrophe: 'Sweete, sacred hill!' (1). Herbert's poems find difficulties in poetic language itself: the 'enchanted groves' (6) and 'purling streams' (8) in 'Jordan [I]' are problematic because they are created fictions; writing about 'heav'nly joyes' (1) in 'Jordan [II]' can lead to obstructively excessive rhetorical devices, which turn back in on themselves as objects of praise ('Curling with metaphors a plain intention' (5)).[35] For Vaughan, however, it is not poetic language but rather the space described which is at issue. Peacham's distinction between a true *topographia* and feigning *topothesia* is brought to bear on an argument about sacred poetry.

'Mount of Olives [I]' demonstrates the role that this literal 'topography' has in a devotional context. The vanity of secular poetry is side-stepped because the location described is directly involved in the history of man's salvation. The Mount will be the 'hill' and 'fountaine' for the poets because 'Their Lord with thee [that is, the Mount] had most to doe' (20):

---

34 See Rudrum's note to the poem in *Henry Vaughan: The Complete Poems*, ed. by Alan Rudrum (Harmondsworth: Penguin, 1976), p. 545.

35 References to Herbert's poetry, provided in the text, are to the text, line numbers and titles in *The English Poems of George Herbert*, ed. by Helen Wilcox (Cambridge: Cambridge University Press, 2007); here, pp. 200, 367. Discussing 'Jordan [I]', Wilcox cites a precedent for Vaughan's reinvention of classical poetry in topographical terms. John Legate's commendatory poem to Christopher Harvey's *The Synagogue; or, The Shadow of the Temple*, 2nd edn (London: J[ohn] L[egate], 1647), suggests that a poet looking to match Herbert's elegance should 'climbe Mount Calvary for Parnassus Hill' (sig. C8v, quoted in *Herbert*, p. 201).

He wept once, walkt whole nights on thee,
And from thence (his suff'rings ended,)
Unto glorie
Was attended[.]
(21-24)

The speaker prescribes a process of 'mind[ing]' (17) the Mount which involves collating its scriptural circumstances: here Luke 19.41 (Christ weeping over Jerusalem), Luke 21.37 (walking before His betrayal), and Acts 1.9 (the Ascension, which Acts 1.12 locates at 'the mount called Olivet').[36] A particular place pins together scriptural cross-references to become a node for understanding the last months of Christ's bodily presence on earth, and a literal point of departure ('from thence') for following and finding Him after His Ascension.

Trying to follow the ascended Christ, however, pushes us beyond our cognitive limitations. The speaker returns to the Mount as a form of epistemological compromise:

Being there [in 'glorie'], this spacious ball
Is but his narrow footstoole all,
And what we thinke
Unsearchable, now with one winke
He doth comprise; But in this aire
When he did stay to beare our Ill
And sinne, this Hill
Was then his Chaire.
(25-32)

Christ is no longer historically present upon earth, and his heavenly perspective is so vertiginous that it exceeds a human understanding of space. The representation of the earth as a 'footstoole' recalls, as Rudrum points out, Isaiah 66.1: 'Thus saith the Lord, The heaven is my throne, and the earth is my footstool'.[37] However, given the other scriptural references, it is perhaps more strongly associated with Stephen's quotation of this passage in Acts 7.49. Stephen is grappling with the problematic location of God on earth: he 'dwelleth not in temples made with hands'; 'what is the place of my rest?', the Lord asks (verses 48, 49). Vaughan's scriptural citations reinforce the epistemological difficulty of locating Christ or God in spatial terms and avoiding idolatry – building a temple oneself

---

36 *Vaughan*, ed. Rudrum, p. 546.
37 *Vaughan*, ed. Rudrum, p. 546.

– in doing so. Turning to a scripturally authorised site where Christ was historically present manages to evade idolatry while securing a degree of theological comprehension. The whole earth is 'Unsearchable'; we lack the cognitive ability to adopt Christ's perspective, and 'comprise' it 'with one winke'. By contrast, the Mount is a manageably sized location which can be reconstructed and productively scrutinised through the lengthier process of scriptural collation described above. This interpretive reassembly of a spatial environment becomes an acceptably non-idolatrous form of reconstituting Christ's presence on earth through scriptural reference while recognising his bodily absence. It was 'in this aire' – still, somehow, a physical witness to Christ's presence – that He 'did stay to beare our Ill / And sinne'.

Transporting oneself to a spatially recreated scriptural location becomes, therefore, a way of breaking the hermeneutic circle: it inscribes transcendent divinity on a locatable site, while at the same time accounting for a compromise in terms of scale (the 'Hill' is Christ's 'Chaire'), and allowing for changes in historical circumstances. This is a form of imaginative reconstruction which operates simultaneously at different levels: it attends to the spatial elements of scriptural scenes, but it is also aware of a broader scriptural narrative and the intervening time between scriptural event and Vaughan's speaker.

Vaughan's conception of sacred geography can be placed in a broader historical context. Locating scriptural events geographically became a pressing concern for sixteenth-century Reformers. The Maps of Canaan which began to appear in German Bibles from the 1520s have been glossed as a reflection of the turn to the literal sense of scripture. Maps provided exegetical assistance because they 'emphasized both the historical reality and the eschatological promise of scripture by demonstrating its geographical setting': like Vaughan's poem, they incorporate transcendent spiritual significance in a specific scriptural location.[38] While Zur Shalev has complicated the confessional reading of this cartographical history, the maps he turns to offer the same essential interpretive formula: the visual medium provides a way of understanding scriptural truths. Shalev identifies a further spiritual use for such examples of *geographica sacra*: maps were intended to be 'devotional images' which allowed the reader to transport him or herself to scriptural locations.[39] Reynolde Wolfe's printer's note to the first English edition of the New Testament with maps stressed the importance of 'Cosmographie' in understanding the 'iourneies of Christ' and 'the Apostles'. A map

---

38 Catherine Delano-Smith and Elizabeth Morley Ingram, *Maps in Bibles 1500-1600: An Illustrated Catalogue*, Travaux d'Humanisme et Renaissance, 256 (Geneva: Droz, 1991), pp. xxi-xxix (p. xxix).

39 Zur Shalev, 'Sacred Geography, Antiquarianism and Visual Erudition: Benito Arias Montano and the Maps in the Antwerp Polyglot Bible', *Imago Mundi*, 55 (2003), 56-80 (p. 67).

of the Mediterranean in the same edition allows us to 'perceaue what peynfull trauayle saynt Paule toke' by calculating the distance he travelled.[40] In all of these instances, topographical representation becomes a way of securing an interpretive foothold on concepts that would otherwise be unquantifiable, whether they are Paul's devotional energy or Christ's Atonement for man's sins. As in Vaughan's poem, the spatial location is not to be 'Idolize[d]' in itself; rather, it is implicated in a hermeneutic process which aims at understanding transhistorical concepts through locatable circumstances. And, of course, a cartographically-based sacred geography is one which is continuously aware of the context of a particular setting. The reader is asked to think him or herself into a scriptural location but also to view it from a spatially transcendent perspective.

In both editions of *Silex Scintillans*, Vaughan's speakers engage in a model of biblical interpretation which reconstructs particular scenes while contextualising them in scripture and in history. Vaughan consistently turns to a reading practice which is similar to that set out by Flacius. However, this process of historicising and collating textual circumstances also creates a central tension in his work. Establishing the context of scriptural locations within scripture and history highlights the hermeneutic limits that inhere in this interaction with the Bible: the sites are problematically distant. Kevin Killeen has suggested that early modern readers found 'omnipresent history' in the scriptures because 'the Bible speaks at multi-temporal levels', and that, through typological interpretations of later historical events, the Bible 'remained a model of utter perspicuity.'[41] It is precisely this idea of 'perspicuity' that is at stake in Vaughan's poetry. Typological reading relies on transhistorical similarities; the Bible is perspicuous because historical specificities of events can be seen through, and commonalities found across all ages. For Vaughan, however, reading scripture often highlights dissimilarities wrought by the chronological and geographical distance between biblical events and his present situation. If read wrongly, the spatial elements of a scriptural scene can radically limit the scriptures' perspicacity, potentially distracting the reader from the true, spiritual sense.

In 'Ascension-day' (*Silex* (1655)) the speaker's ascent 'Up to the skies' (10) is, paradoxically, structured through a variety of earth-bound biblical locations. From a transcendent perspective, eschatological scenes are grafted onto various scriptural sites: he 'greet[s] [Christ's] sepulchre and . . . Grave' (15); he sees, 'at the last great day' (29), 'Saints and Angels' who 'glorifie the earth' (26); and, returning

40 *The Newe Testament: Translated by Myles Couerdale, and conferred with W. Tyndales translation* (London: Reynolde Wolfe, 1549), title page verso, sig. Z8r. Quoted and glossed in Delano-Smith and Morley Ingram, pp. xxiv-xxv.

41 Kevin Killeen, 'Chastising with Scorpions: Reading the Old Testament in Early Modern England', *Huntington Library Quarterly*, 73 (2010), 491-506 (pp. 493, 495, 497).

to the setting of the Ascension, he can 'walk the fields of *Bethani*' (37). The speaker can find Christ on earth by traversing a series of mentally recreated locations: 'With these fair thoughts I move in this fair place, / And the last steps of my milde Master trace' (49-50). But, as the process of 'trac[ing]' suggests, this is an act of following and writing a set of events which has already happened; Christ's presence, in this instance, cannot be textually recaptured. At the moment of Christ's Ascension (when 'the cloud doth now receive [Him]' (57)), Vaughan, like the apostles (and all humankind since then), loses 'sight' (57) of Him – only, of course, he has never seen Him. In His place are the 'two men' (58) of Acts 1.10, who prophesy Christ's return (Acts 1.11), and who, in accordance with Christ's interpretation of Jewish law to the Pharisees (John 8.17), bear verifiable witness to the Ascension. The speaker's journey through scriptural locations has reached an epistemological limit. He collates the spatial circumstances of Christ's 'last steps', but, when it comes to ascending with Christ himself, he can only turn to further textual testimony (the prophecy of 'the two men') and appeal to the now absent Christ to return as a 'faithful witness' (61), precisely because the speaker is unable to see Christ at first hand.

Vaughan's speaker can also, however, turn beyond Acts to Paul's accounts of the Holy Spirit's testimony. 'The Spirit itself beareth witness with our spirit' (Romans 8.16); those Ephesians who 'trusted' Christ, 'heard the word of truth' and 'believed' were 'sealed with that holy Spirit of promise' (Ephesians 1.13). In 'Ascension-day', the Spirit, continuing to act on a speaker who is himself diligently reading 'the word of truth', seals his faith in Christ's Ascension and the future promise of his part in Christ's 'victory':

> Thy glorious, bright Ascension (though remov'd
> So many Ages from me) is so prov'd
> And by thy Spirit seal'd to me, that I
> Feel me a sharer in thy victory.
> (5-8)

Turning to historical situations where Christ walked is only a step on the path to understanding. Collating and imagining ancient scriptural sites can only accrue a limited sense of plausibility; instead, God's grace, in spite of historical distance ('So many Ages'), 'prov[es]' a visually imagined event ('glorious, bright') through 'feel[ing]'. Vaughan requires a supplementary testimony from the Holy Spirit because the process of collating and reimagining events can only take us so far; it is problematically earth-bound and limited by historical distance. For, despite Vaughan's antipathy to radical claims for direct spiritual revelation (typified by

the 'new lights' (9) in 'White Sunday' (*Silex* (1655))),[42] the continuing interven-
tion of the Spirit in Vaughan's own historical context is a governing trope for
Silex Scintillans. The transformation of the poet's 'stony heart' to 'flesh' by God's
hand, depicted in the emblematic frontispiece of the first edition, is also a process
of receiving a 'new spirit' from the Lord (Ezekiel 36.26).

The epistemological problems and interpretive limits involved in imaginatively
reconstructing scriptural locations can help us understand one of Vaughan's
most problematic poems, 'The Search' (*Silex* (1650)). This poem has been interpreted by various critics as an attempt on Vaughan's part to theorise modes of
reading and meditation.[43] In a similar vein, I want to suggest that it engages
directly with the model of recreating historical locations. It enunciates the
problems inherent in this interpretive method, and dramatises the difficulties
that the speaker faces in turning to different means of experiencing and understanding God.

Vaughan's speaker, as in the *Mount of Olives*, enters a selection of scriptural
scenes 'To find [his] Saviour' (5): he travels 'As far as *Bethlem*' (6), 'To *Egypt*' (11),
'to *Sychar*' (21), and to '*Jacobs wel*' (22). Instead of finding Christ in these places,
he is made continuously aware of the time-lapse between his own historical
context and the scenes he wishes to find. The '*Temple*' (15), where he hopes to
find Christ preaching, is 'A little dust, and . . . the Town / A heap of ashes' (16-17).
The speaker has arrived too late; the Temple was destroyed in CE 70. In his
Life of Paulinus, Vaughan compares the abolition of feast days in 1645 with the
(to his mind) desecration of the 'Two places upon Earth . . . most renowned
with the memory of our Saviour, *Bethlem* for his *birth*, and mount *Calvarie* for
his *passion*': a '*Mosquie*' and an 'Idol of *Jupiter*' have been set up in their
place.[44] The reconstruction of these sites in 'The Search' is made impossible by
these historical changes. Moreover, anachronistic interventions point the speaker
in the wrong direction: there is a 'Monument' at Christ's grave 'For he had
none' (46). A legible artefact commemorating Christ in fact negates its own
signifying function: it informs the speaker of Christ's absence. Its 'undefil'd,
and new-heaw'd' (47) state is doubly problematic because on the one hand it is
clearly a later addition, and therefore inauthentic, but on the other its anachronic-
ity is only evident because it fails to signify the historical lapse – the wear over
time – that the speaker attempts to overcome. The synchronic difficulty of
finding Christ in His own time and in relation to one's own circumstances is

42 See West, pp. 170-73.

43 Lewalski (p. 335) presents it as a criticism of Catholic models of meditation; Michael Srigley,
'Ritual Entries: Some Approaches to Henry Vaughan's 'Silex Scintillans'', *Scintilla*, 3 (1999), 43-59,
sees it as 'an allegory of right and wrong reading' (p. 58).

44 Vaughan, *Works*, p. 379.

made apparent. After an extensive search, the speaker notes the various locations he 'should rove in, and rest [his] head / Where my deare Lord did often tread' (71-72). But this is also an interpretive pitfall. One of the key biblical passages implied by the poem is Matthew 8.18-22, in which the 'certain scribe' asks to 'follow' Christ (verse 19): Jesus replies that 'the Son of man hath not where to lay his head' (verse 20). The speaker (another 'scribe') is misguided on two counts. He does not attend to the scriptural context of his searches: the implicit allusion to Matthew 8 ironically demonstrates the speaker's interpretive oversight of this passage; he follows Christ mistakenly by looking for somewhere to 'rest'. More generally, the speaker's method of 'follow[ing]' is a problematically over-literal interpretation of a command (Matthew 4.19) which, in his historical context, can only be spiritually fulfilled.

At the end of this journey, the speaker 'heard one singing' (74). A voice intervenes with a hymn that tells him to 'Leave . . . thy gadding thoughts' (75), to move his attention from 'out of Doores' (78) inwards, past 'The skinne, and shell of things' (81), and away from the historical sites ('old Elements, / or Dust' (88-89)) where he has attempted to find Christ. But this is also a move upwards – the focus on specious materiality is 'got / By meer Despair / of wings' (85-87). At precisely the moment when we expect directional instructions, the speaker is presented with total deictic confusion, told to 'Search . . . another world' (95), and only given a definition of the 'way' (93) that should not be taken. This directional ambiguity is, perhaps, explained by the quotation from Acts 17.27-28 which ends the poem: we should 'feel after' God; he is 'not far off from every one of us'. The passage is taken from Paul's sermon at the Areopagus in which he instructs the Athenians not to conceive of God as inhering in a particular physical location: echoing Stephen, Paul states that God 'dwelleth not in temples made with hands' (verse 24). Vaughan is not, I think, denying the possibility that the reimagined scriptural places his speaker searches contain some traces of Christ's presence, or that spaces themselves can be sanctified. As Andrew Spicer has shown, the exegesis of Paul's admonition in the context of ecclesiological debates allowed seventeenth-century preachers to condemn allegedly excessive Roman Catholic liturgical ritual while maintaining a qualified notion of sacred space.[45] God could still come to a particular holy place without being wrongly perceived as limited by the place's materiality. In an analogous argument, Vaughan rejects an over-literalistic form of reading which fixes Christ's presence in the potentially idolatrous elements of scriptural scene, while still allowing a more modest form of searching to take place. This search is only

---

45 See Andrew Spicer, 'Holiness and *The Temple*: Thomas Adams and the Definition of Sacred Space in Jacobean England', *The Seventeenth Century*, 27 (2012), 1-24. For quotations of Acts 17.24, see pp. 7-8.

permissible if it accepts the limitations of its method. It must leave room for grace to direct the reader to find Christ's timeless meaning as eternal Saviour, which is not restricted either to historical sites or to their imaginatively recreated forms. As the intervening voice suggests, these directions cannot be translated into practicable instructions that operate at a spatial level (moving upwards, through, or inwards), because the ultimate goal sought by the reader transcends space and time itself: no matter where we are, God is never far off. Searching for Christ in scripture is valuable, but only if it is part of a longer process. Readers must wait for grace to take them past the 'old Elements' to a spiritual apprehension of God.

Vaughan's intervening voice also authorises another modest form of tracing through textual structures. The 'singing' voice that guides the speaker is an allusion to the spoken interventions in Herbert's poetry. In 'Jordan [II]', for example, the speaker

> might heare a friend
> Whisper, *How wide is all this long pretence!*
> *There is in love a sweetnesse readie penn'd:*
> *Copie out onely that, and save expense.*
> (15-18)

In the same way that the intervening voice in Herbert's poetry reinvents Sidney's 'looke in thy heart and write' into a cryptic instruction for the devotional poet,[46] Vaughan's citation of Herbert's poetic technique provides him with a set of obscure directions just at the point when turning to places in scripture becomes a methodological failure. But citing Herbert is, at least, another way of 'trac[ing]' an established path. As the preface to *Silex Scintillans* (1655) explains, others have 'followed' Herbert '*Sed non passibus aequis*' – 'but with steps that match not his'.[47] Vaughan, quoting Virgil, again resituates classical poetics in a Christian context. Following in Herbert's footsteps, rather than Christ's, provides an alternative, poetic structure for finding God.

---

46 Sir Philip Sidney, *Astrophil and Stella*, I.14, in *The Poems of Sir Philip Sidney*, ed. by William A. Ringler, Jr. (Oxford: Clarendon Press, 1962), p. 165. Wilcox notes Herbert's 'parody' of this line (*Herbert*, p. 370).

47 Vaughan, *Works*, p. 391, quoting Virgil, *Aeneid*, II.724 (translated *Vaughan*, ed. Rudrum, p. 528).

'Clouds'
by Christopher Werrett

RUTH BIDGOOD

Extremes

Out of shade, the track
ran down to a shimmering house,
glare of white walls, utmost
rigour of heat. In a treeless field
a solitary pony looked stunned,
motionless except for grudged effort
of draggle-tail swish at flies.

We had inched the car under trees
and sat on the bank, torpid, plan-less.
I had known other seasons here–
spring with mild warmth gentling the land,
small clear bird – notes, quiet light;
autumn's drama and its gift
of returning vistas, hills framed by branches
when vivid leaves fall.

But today, extreme bred extreme.
I sensed through heavy stillness of heat
a deeper silence of winter; envisioned
dark daytime skies, weird uniformity
of white, with its own chill glare,
transforming field after field,
climbing and capping distant hills,
outlawing for long
the vocabulary of thaw.

Today's reality and imagining
were alike savage – maybe the truest mode
of apprehending a countryside
always beautiful, rarely benign;
where extremes stubbornly claim inalienable
rights of return.

Making May

May, when Lucifer fell, they say:
when wolves are born.
May, anciently
the unlucky month
of hawthorn spells,
of chill taboo,
unchosen chastity.

Then metamorphosis,
hawthorn asserting
scent of the female,
devotees half-smothered
in sheaves of it, flung
in whirling dance
that caressed the towering pole.

Where now are those contraries?
Have they blended to make
this May of ours, flowing in dappled ease
along a road under arch after arch
of green-gold boughs?
                        Nothing here
of barren deprivation. Down each dip
of the road, round every curve, there comes
a soft echo of dancing elation.

Triptych

(suggested by photographs in Phil Cope's 'Borderlands')

1. Portrait of a Devotee

The well-seeker has found her pool,
unobtrusive but sacred.
She stands in contemplation,
head bowed towards the brownish
gently stirring water, hands lightly clasped,
not so much in prayer as modestly
suggesting that state.

It isn't easy here to be sure
of the feeder-stream's course - towards
the well it mazily wambles,
now visible, now half-hidden in clumps
of wetland foliage. From the pool
there starts a rocky tumble down
to join a flow more definite
than anything in this upland place.

Behind the tussock where the woman stands,
seen past her shoulder,
both trunks of a split tree are presences,
each lifting out to either side
branches upturning like a pair of wings.

2. Oswald's Well

A sweep of wild common, green
broken by long straw-like grass,
tinged with red by the well
of a martyred king – as though
there is never quite an end
to Penda's butchery.

A hole like a black grave; water
unseen – inadequate fencing
makes no attempt at symmetry.
Far off, one stark house stares.

What in the picture makes
the most insistent claim
on our eyes? Is it
the solitary house, that should spell
humankind, normality, yet offers nothing
of reassurance?
                         Or the profound hole
of the well, cancelling sight
in black deeps?
                         Or is it the line
of hedgerow trees, echoing
the hurry of driven clouds
over a livid sky? Some trees are too short
to feel the strenuous wind's assault,
yet in their sombre bushiness
seem not at rest.
                         What of the taller ones?
Go, go, go! shouts the wind,
and they strain to obey, lurching
forward, away, as is hating their own
rootedness, that allows no escape.

Escape? Perhaps there is none here
for anything – distant staring house;
Sky, huge, disturbed; well-water
lurking in blackness; boundary – trees
vainly struggling away from fear;
land uneasy, tainted with blood
unredemptive, never wholly
soaking away.

3. The Yew

Young when the Romans left? The pictured yew
seems older than that – not constrained
at all by time.

                     Its grip on the hill
is passionate. Its massive bulk
suggests excess. The trunk, with it harsh bark,
is composite – knots, ridges, bulges, looking tortured,
are flung together and meld.
Branches are of fearful proportion,
obscure patterns of growth.

                       Some, at the brink
of the hill, have a rushing movement, cling
close to the slope, as though caressing it,
follow it down to an unseen well.

The tree is garlanded, swollen mossy limbs
flaunting red ribbons and white, a dangling heart,
a hotchpotch of offerings from givers
who come to weep, thank, celebrate, implore;
who have some sense, perhaps, of the great yew's
terrible love of transient earth, of its fierce craving
to stay for ever clutching the hill,
for ever sweeping down to hidden waters;
as if it longs, and knows the longing vain,
for a gnarled, rooted, earthbound eternity.

PRUE CHAMBERLAYNE

How Beauty Travels

Our ice-age ancestors
loved beauty, depicted rippling backs of bison,
felt intimate with the immense.

This was refined at Lindisfarne
in artistry pricked on vellum – Coptic patterns,
Celtic curls in lapis lazuli and malachite,
ink of fish glue, soot, egg-white.

From his rock Cuthbert watched
blaze from puddled mud out-dazzle evening sky,
sand ribs meticulously ploughed by currents,
deep runnels revealed at furthest ebb.

Listened to seals, querulous but conversational,
stepped between barnacles and wormcasts,
made rosaries from devils' toenails – ringed crinoids
of the tropics – still scattered on the beach.

He chose a walled cell open to the sky.

Duplex Emulation:
George Herbert's "Christmas" &
Henry Vaughan's "Christ's Nativity"

JONATHAN NAUMAN

George Herbert's duplex poems commemorating the principal feasts of the Christian year, "Easter"[1] and "Christmas" (292), seem especially to have stirred Henry Vaughan's well-known desire to emulate the author of *The Temple*. We find in *Silex Scintillans* a poem for "Easter-Day"[2] followed by an "Easter-Hymn" (216) and a poem for "Ascension-Day" (243-245) followed by an "Ascension-Hymn" (245-246), sequences which seem straightforwardly to answer Herbert's sacred incitement in the second part of his lyric "Christmas":

> The shepherds sing; and shall I silent be?
> My God, no hymne for thee? (ll. 15-16)

None of Vaughan's replies to Herbert's holy day performances, however, matches the intense complex of interactions pursued in the duplex *Silex Scintillans* lyric on "Christ's Nativity" (199-200). Let us read Herbert's Christmas poem, and then Vaughan's, in order to track the implications of Vaughan's literary response.

Formally, the first movement of Herbert's "Christmas" is a sonnet; but its opening lines sound more like a ballad preparing to recount a series of yuletide adventures:

> All after pleasures as I rid one day,
> My horse and I, both tir'd, bodie and minde,

---

1 Helen Wilcox, ed., *The English Poems of George Herbert* (Cambridge: Cambridge University Press, 2007), pp. 139-140. All following references to Herbert's works will be cited within my text from this edition.

2 Alan Rudrum, ed., *Henry Vaughan: The Complete Poems* (Harmondsworth, Middlesex: Penguin Books, 1976 [1983]), pp. 215-216. All following references to Vaughan's works will be cited within my text from this edition.

With full crie of affections, quite astray,
I took up in the next inne I could finde.

There when I came, whom found I but my deare (ll. 1-5)

— and for the moment, let us stop! In the next line — line six — the poem will suddenly change from a parable of profanity to an encounter with the incarnate Christ; and this change will be especially sharpened by repeated use of two forms of the word "deare," which substantive here has been drawn by the hunting idiom "full crie" (l. 3)[3] toward an animal meaning; it has also been drawn toward undisciplined erotism by "all after pleasures" (l. 1), "affections" (l. 3), and the casual opportunism of "the next inne I could finde" (l. 4). But just when "deare" intensifies to "dearest," we meet the "Lord":

There when I came, whom found I but my deare,
    My dearest Lord, expecting till the grief
    Of pleasures brought me to him, readie there
To be all passengers most sweet relief?
O Thou, whose glorious, yet contracted light,
    Wrapt in nights mantle, stole into a manger;
    Since my dark soul and brutish is thy right,
To man of all beasts be not thou a stranger:
    Furnish & deck my soul, that thou mayst have
    A better lodging then a rack or grave. (ll. 5-14)

The profane yule episode is transformed: there was no room for Christ in line four's "inne"! And as Helen Wilcox has pointed out (293), Herbert's unusual intransitive use of "expecting" in line six recalls testimony in the *Epistle to the Hebrews* to Christ seated at "the right hand of God, from henceforth expecting till his enemies be made his footstool" (Heb. 10:12-13, A.V.).[4] Romance narrative verse becomes a sonnet, haphazard heroic adventure submits to the expectations of the Divine Hero, and we end in a completely different kind of inn, with the repentant speaker offering his own soul for Christ's lodging.

What the first movement of Herbert's "Christmas" does with episodic romance, the second movement does with classical pastoral.

The shepherds sing; and shall I silent be?
My God, no hymn for thee? (ll. 15-16)

---

3 Wilcox, p. 293.
4 This passage recalls Ps. 110:1, cited by Jesus as proof of the Divine nature of the Messiah (Luke 20:41-44).

Herbert's gesture toward singing shepherds may bring first to mind, in this context, the Biblical shepherds who, after witnessing the birth of the Christ Child, "returned, glorifying and praising God for all the things that they had heard and seene" (Luke 2:20, A.V.); but it should be noted that St. Luke's shepherds are not specifically said to be singing. Emulative song was, however, a known and ubiquitous practice in "the singing contests of classical pastoral."[5] Naturally one need not press the distinction so far as to exclude any attempt on Herbert's part to emulate the Biblical shepherds here; but the rhetoric of the preceding sonnet and the ensuing gestures of the second movement seem particularly concerned with redirecting classical, literary, and yuletide-pagan conventions toward Christian devotion. Thus, the methodical redeployment of pastoral and celebratory yuletide images in the lines that follow:

> My soul's a shepherd too; a flock it feeds
> Of thoughts, and words, and deeds.
> The pasture is thy word: the streams, thy grace
> Enriching all the place.
> Shepherd and flock shall sing, and all my powers
> Out-sing the day-light houres.
> Then we will chide the sunne for letting night
> Take up his place and right:
> We sing one common Lord; wherefore he should
> Himself the candle hold. (ll. 17-26)

Through his deliberate allegory, Herbert has turned his yuletide celebration into a dynamic of the soul seeking perpetually to honor the Lord, an endeavor found in turn to be incompatible with the variable natural sun, especially in its brief appearances in winter. The poet must therefore have recourse once more to allegory, though not as straightforwardly as in the case of shepherd, flock, and pasture.

> I will go searching, till I finde a sunne
> Shall stay, till we have done;
> A willing shiner, that shall shine as gladly
> As frost-nipt sunnes look sadly.
> Then we will sing, and shine all our own day,
> And one another pay:
> His beams shall cheer my breast, and both so twine,
> Till ev'n his beams sing, and my musick shine. (ll. 27-34)

---

5 Neil Curry and Natasha Curry, *George Herbert* (London: Greenwich Exchange, 2010), p. 72.

Herbert's new, supernatural sun, his "willing shiner," gestures toward the incarnate and glorified Christ – the sun / Son pairing seems inevitable – and its effects emerge as a spiritual presence in the "breast" of the poet, fully granting (as Chauncey Wood has said) the plea for God to "cheer and tune my heartlesse breast" in the preceding poem, "Deniall" (288-289).[6] The second movement of Herbert's Christmas poem, his allegorically adjusted eclogue, thus ends analogously with his divinely redirected narrative romance – i.e., with a dynamic spiritual transformation within the speaker.

When we pass from George Herbert's sacred poetic vision to Henry Vaughan's, as many readers have noticed, we pass (in the episcopal Anglican point-of-view) from stable Jacobean and Carolean establishment to impassioned memory of earlier Anglican days amidst an apparent downward spiral of ecclesiastical and political defeat. The impetus behind Vaughan's emulation of Herbert's double lyric on the Christmas holy day is primarily devotional and literary, with commentary on current events emerging in "Christ's Nativity" only in the second movement. There is, however, a modification of mood, a difference from Herbert in approach throughout Vaughan's poem which probably does indicate Vaughan's engagements with the Welsh Puritan insurgency. While Herbert's "Christmas" delivers thoughtful and pointed sacred answers to popular and pagan-classicist literary traditions, Vaughan's Nativity poem emerges from a Laudian affirmation of aesthetics and ceremony, a Christian-hermetist perception of God's presence in the natural world, and a sharp personal consciousness of having licentiously misused his own lyrical powers in earlier work. These are gradients to keep in mind as we observe the end of Herbert's "Christmas" providing a starting point for Vaughan's "Christ's Nativity," whose opening finds the poet singing on Christ's birthday in concert with the "Sun."

> Awake, glad heart! get up, and sing,
> It is the Birth-day of thy King,
>   Awake! awake!
>   The Sun doth shake
> Light from his locks, and all the way
> Breathing perfumes, doth spice the day.
>
> 2.
> Awake, awake! hark, how the *wood* rings,
> *Winds* whisper, and the busy *springs*

6 Chauncey Wood, "Configuring Herbert's 'Christmas,'" *George Herbert Journal* 17.ii (1994): 21-35.

A consort make;
Awake, awake!
Man is their high-priest, and should rise
To offer up the sacrifice.

3.
I would I were some *bird*, or star,
Fluttering in woods, or lifted far
    Above this *inn*
    And road of sin!
Then either star, or *bird*, should be
Shining, or singing still to thee. (ll. 1-18)

As readers of Herbert and Vaughan have pointed out,[7] these opening stanzas of "Christ's Nativity" echo one Herbert poem after another. The description of Vaughan's rising sun recalls the "light" and "perfume" of sunrise in Herbert's duplex "Easter" (139-140),[8] which is also one source of Vaughan's repeated imperative "Awake!"[9] Vaughan hearkens, as Herbert does in the opening lines of "Mans medley" (458-459) to "how the birds do sing, / And woods do ring"; and he dramatically endorses Herbert's figuring of man's role in Creation from the fourth stanza of Herbert's "Providence" (416-421):

Man is the worlds high Priest: he doth present
The sacrifice for all; while they below
Unto the service mutter an assent,
Such as springs use that fall, and windes that blow. (ll. 13-16)

Something is lost in this *a fortiori* emulation, in which not just the sun, but woods, winds, springs, birds, and stars join Herbert's anticipated cheer, "shining, or singing still to thee," viz., the whimsical subtlety of Herbert's gesture toward Christology and incarnational *synergeia* in his hypothetical duet with the "sunne." But something is also gained when we pass from Herbert's irenic and perspi-

---

7 See Rudrum's notes (p. 565) and also L. C. Martin, ed., *The Works of Henry Vaughan*, 2nd ed. (Oxford: Clarendon Press, 1957), p. 758, and also Louis L. Martz, ed., *Henry Vaughan: Selected Poems* (Oxford and New York: Oxford University Press, 1995), p. 192.

8 In Herbert's poem, however, the natural splendors of many springtime sunrises are being contrasted with the one Resurrection of Christ: the natural sun, "though he give light, & th'East perfume," cannot compare with the supernatural human life witnessed to by the Church on Easter. When Vaughan translates the chronological location of Herbert's "Light" and "perfume" from Easter to Christmas, the significances of the images migrate closer to the supernatural.

9 See also "The Dawning" (112) for the double imperative, "Awake, awake" (l. 5).

cacious wit to Vaughan's enthusiastic sacred literary performance, his expansive celebration of nature's response to God. The Herbertian echoes give an impression, not of carefully thought out literary allusion, but of visionary descant (observe the exclamation marks!), and Vaughan's ceremony takes his audience far above the "*inn* / And road of sin" that Herbert depicts in order to interrupt. As Irene Shewell Cooper once said, Vaughan has the "power of bridging, with a word or sentence, the gulf between the kingdom of this world and the Kingdom of Heaven, so that the gulf becomes as if it had never been."[10]

Cooper later mentions a certain flaw often attributed to Henry Vaughan, that of bathos; and she suggests that, in some cases in *Silex Scintillans*, bathos actually becomes a strength, a bold willingness to set God's goodness "over against man's littleness."[11] It is the best literary argument I've heard for appreciating the sudden descent into self-accusation in the last two stanzas of the first movement of "Christ's Nativity." In terms of Vaughan's emulation of Herbert, these lines emerge from the preceding stanza's gesture toward Herbert's unsanctified yule-season "*inn*," and they act as an intense testimonial amplification of the concluding motives of Herbert's sonnet.

> 4.
> I would I had in my best part
> Fit rooms for thee! or that my heart
> Were so clean as
> Thy manger was!
> But I am all filth, and obscene,
> Yet, if thou wilt, thou canst make clean.
>
> 5.
> Sweet *Jesu*! will then; let no more
> This leper haunt, and soil thy door,
> Cure him, ease him
> O release him!
> And let once more by mystick birth
> The Lord of life be born in Earth. (ll. 19-30)

Vaughan's repentant finale, intensified with repetition and internal rhyme,[12] returns even more explicitly than Herbert's Christmas poem conclusions to the

---

10 "The Religious Genius of Henry Vaughan," *Theology* 32 (May, 1936): 294-297.

11 *Ibid.*

12 Jonathan Post spotlights this passage as a prime example of Vaughan's ability to develop galvanizing sound effects in his stanza forms; see *Henry Vaughan: The Unfolding Vision* (Princeton, NJ: Princeton University Press, 1982), p. 91.

Birth of Christ and the spiritual transformations that event can enable. This combination of celebration, penitence, and renewed focus on the personal effects of the Incarnation has also a public declamatory force that would have been considered defiant at its publication in 1650, some years after Parliament had voted to forbid public and ecclesiastical celebrations of Easter and Christmas.[13] Certainly Vaughan knew that his enactment of a Christmas celebration whose harmony with nature led to penitence would controvert Parliament's description of liturgical festivals as mere occasions for pagan relapse and moral decadence. Vaughan was no Herrick: he actually shared the Puritans' concerns about degenerate Christmas celebrations, and would later print a poem entitled "The true Christmas" (374) denouncing those who would "stick up *ivy* and the *bays*, / And then restore the *heathen* ways" (ll. 1-2), hosting Christmas parties with yuletide riot and senseless extravagance.[14] But such moral seriousness only sharpened his dissent against Parliament's removal of Church customs that he had experienced as bulwarks against worldliness and vice.

The second movement of "Christ's Nativity" rhetorically mirrors the second movement of Herbert's "Christmas" by passing from personal dialogue with the Lord Christ to dramatic exhortation, except that in Vaughan, Herbert's challenging questions – "shall I silent be? / My God, no hymne for thee?" – do not move on to allegory or figure: the questions follow one after another, building toward an impassioned indictment of the Puritan regime for its opposition to holy festivals.

> How kind is heaven to man! If here
> One sinner doth amend
> Straight there is joy, and every sphere
> In music doth contend;
> And shall we then no voices lift?
> Are mercy, and salvation
> Not worth our thanks? Is life a gift
> Of no more acceptation?
> Shall he that did come down from thence
> And here for us was slain,

---

13 As Philip West notes, Parliament began to prohibit Church festivals "in 1645, when traditional celebration of Christmas was forbidden; by June 1647 Easter, Whitsun, and Rogationtide had followed Christmas into the Act book"; see *Henry Vaughan's* Silex Scintillans: *Scripture Uses* (Oxford and London: Oxford University Press, 2001), p. 148.

14 Vaughan especially takes to task a hostess whose holiday theatrics, "gallant *furniture*," and ostentatious dinner plate (ll. 12-13) seem to him incommensurate with nature's mortification at winter solstice and "the *Manger's* mean Estate" (l. 14); and he advises that she would do better to forsake "wild *revels,* and loose *hall*" (l. 6) and "Dress finely what comes not in sight" (l. 27).

> Shall he be now cast off? no sense
>   Of all his woes remain?
> Can neither love, nor sufferings bind?
>   Are we all stone, and earth?
> Neither his bloody passions mind,
>   Nor one day bless his birth?
> Alas, my God! Thy birth now here
> Must not be numbered in the year. (II. ll. 1-18)

There is reason to think that this Laudian tirade did not go without its desired challenging effect. More than two centuries later, when interest in Vaughan's texts began to revive in the aftermath of the Romantic movement, Alexander Grosart, a clergyman with Whig loyalties[15] and one of Vaughan's pioneering editors would inveigh against Vaughan's sentiments in his commentary on this passage: "there can be nothing but pity for the stupid bigotry that refuses to recognize deeper motive than mere destructiveness in such obliteration of the celebration of Christmas-day," he said.[16] But Henry Vaughan was in fact, like Herbert, fully cognizant of the "deeper" spiritual problems that preoccupied the Puritan movement – heartlessness and superstition, discrepancies between professed religious motives and ambitions toward various forms of worldly prestige and gain. His polemics, however, would associate these failings with the Welsh Puritans themselves and with their replacement liturgies. Just as Herbert sought to surprise his classically-trained audience into greater reverence for the mystery of the Incarnation, Vaughan – in his very different, politically-contested situation – sought to reinforce his audience's sense of surrounding holiness in the external world, and to choreograph good use of the dynamics of nature and the Christian year in support of traditional sacramental worship.

---

15 Grosart dedicated his Vaughan edition to Gladstone's Solicitor General, interjecting adulatory comments about the incoming Whig government as he did so. See *The Works of Verse and Prose Complete of Henry Vaughan, Silurist*, 4 vols. (St. Georges, Blackburn, Lancashire: Printed for private circulation, 1871), I.iv.

16 Grosart, II.xliii.

'Small Waterfall'
by Christopher Werrett

WILLIAM VIRGIL DAVIS

His Life

– after Frank Bidart

There had been a time, a time ago,
when no one would have known what his life

would become, where it would go.
They would have said he had all of his life

ahead of him. He too often wondered
what he would make of his life.

Early on, he was anxious to find out.
Later, when he thought back over his life,

he had trouble making much sense of it.
He asked others what they thought his life

signified – if anything. They lied,
or were polite. Didn't he see that his life

had been "full," blessed"? They
all said they envied him his life

and would, if they could, have happily
traded their lives for his life,

that he ought to appreciate it.
When he started to write the story of his life

he didn't know where to begin,
but he began, "His life . . ."

Some of them wondered
if he would be sorry he had taken his life.

A Sonnet for Paul Muldoon

Pigs and trees, stars and horses – how many are
we to count before the whole lot lets go,
and the next thing you know
they are all running down a hill toward a yard-
like meadow just above a cliff,
above a view, above the old ocean beating itself
up over an old love lost or some rough shelf
sticking up from the deep shift
of wind and keeping
an eye out for anything in the area
whether we care about it or not, Sarah.
And so, you see, I'll go on singing
about earth, air, fire and water or
pigs and trees and stars and horses, brother.

Departures

I misread Thomas Kinsella's line
Endure and let the present punish as
"Endure and let the present perish."

There was, I think, good reason
for my misreading, since it was
followed by a line that would work

equally well with either reading:
Looking backward, all is lost.
Kinsella, of course, was thinking

of Ireland and a past that no one
not there could ever pray to know.
I was thinking of Lord knows what,

my own past I guess, and my future,
anything to escape the immediate
moment, sitting here on the last

day of the third month, wondering
what will happen next, and realizing
that I was *a man of the moment of*

departure, turning to leave, but going
somewhere, and hoping to do
something, before being punished

or perishing.

"Woman with Her Hair Tousled by the Wind in Front of an Eclipse"

– after the painting by Miró

She is facing both ways at once. The ant-like antennae
on her head, balanced like barbells, hold her down
while everything around her churns and spins in circles.
One side of the sun, fixed above her head, is red,
tipped with a curved black triangle at its top. The other
side is lost in the eclipse. Below this Stephen Crane
red sun pasted in the sky is a smeared ghostly moon
above a spider-webbed, eight-pointed stick-star floating
in space over a monocycle running away on its own.
To the right, near the edge of the frame, are double
handles and another thin barbell holding what might
be the woman's unloosened eyes, fallen free from her
head but held on slender strings. Her face, like a Rothko,
is yellow over green, implying the illumination possible
in a ruminative mind over a negative base. There are
two other circles unaccounted for at the far right, one
large and dripping, solid and black, set at the vertical
center, the other a faint purple, and lower, almost off
the edge of the canvas, mirroring the large gray moon
on the other side, half-hidden by the red sun and one
side of the woman's head. Everything here suggests
that, very soon, the whole world will disappear.

JOHN FREEMAN

A First Visit to Steep

That morning's news had been of six young soldiers
killed by a roadside bomb in Afghanistan.
From the car I glimpsed the war memorial
with a bouquet of artificial poppies,
perhaps left and renewed all through the year,
or placed there last Saturday or Sunday,
March the third or fourth. Start the walk near the church,
said the guide, and here was the church, but oh,
here were a group of people wearing black,
a young man with a strong, sensitive face
trying not to cry, but not succeeding.
It was as if we had to approach this place
of so much life through the lych-gate of death,
and it seemed fitting that it should be so.

He fell a year short of seeing forty.
Carrying that knowledge lightly as we walked,
I felt his companionship, a young man's,
a young fit man's, as I toiled up the hill
he would have bounded up, no doubt, except
when he was kept in by a twisted ankle
and for the first time got stuck into writing
poems after a million words of prose.
His time was short, and so was ours on the walk,
so is mine writing this now, and I could not,
even with more, do justice to the walk,
which didn't do justice to the place. I want
to go back, but it won't be the first time,
with all the specialness of the first time.

Birds sang for the entire two hours, robins,
blackbirds, finches, and above all thrushes,
especially towards the end, and once each
we heard an owl and a drumming woodpecker.

The air is so pure that lichen flourishes
on the bark of trees, and the fallen logs
were covered over with a thick fur of moss.
There was a stand of snowdrops at the top
of the hill where we turned along the ridge,
and past The Red House where the poet lived,
as well as in the cottages far below.
The views coming down Shoulder of Mutton Hill
were panoramic, lush, and glorious,
just as the poem 'Wind and Mist' describes.
The memorial is unobtrusive,
dignified. My joints ached, which was my tribute,
like lighting a candle, to put me in tune
with the quotation set into the stone:
and I rose up and knew that I was tired
and continued my journey. Back at the church
the mourners were gone, and I went through the gate.

John Davies of Hereford, the King of Denmark & Shakespeare's Meeting of Kings: Praise Beyond Praise

JOSEPH STERRETT

In many ways Peter was my academic father. He was not my supervisor, nor was he directly in my field. But, always congenial and encouraging, he observed my work from those very rough days as a new PhD student wrestling with too many ideas, trying to make sensible shape out of them. He taught, or rather showed me how to edit. He was a 'strong' editor – 'strong' in the sense that he had no hesitation in rearranging and reorganising another writer's work to make it read more clearly or to get the ideas to flow more logically in the argument. We edited *Sacred Text-Sacred Space* together, a surprising outcome from a small bursary and a back-of-the-envelope postgraduate idea. With *Scintilla* I had been helping here and there since 12, but *Scintilla 16* was our first jointly edited issue, a moment when many thought the journal would retire. Much of what I could say has been better said by others who knew him longer, but looking through my emails as I prepared to go to his funeral, it was clear that he was the person with whom I had had the most correspondence over the previous five or six years: more than family, more than any other friend. We never said goodbye. (How can you?) Instead, through frequent, brief phone conversations and continued steady emails, we carefully and deliberately moved the systems, the accounts, and the vision of *Scintilla* into other hands. And then came the day in early September 2014 when I phoned about a small detail and no one answered. This was unusual for either he or Lucienne was always home. I have to confess, death is something I do not really understand. I don't really know what to feel or how to behave at funerals. What I did feel was that moment nearly a year later – after the horror of Anne's passing, after the whirlwind of my own brush with finality – when I looked at the everyday matters needed for the running of *Scintilla* and wanted so very much to call him or email just to chat about what had to be done. What follows is the conclusion of a conversation I had many times with Peter over the last few years of his life about a poem by a not very well known poet who identified himself as a man from the borders of Wales. Peter, you are missed.

On the evening of July 17, 1606, seven 'goodly tal shippes' bearing the Danish King sailed up the River Thames and cast anchor at Gravesend.[1] Here, a 'warlike' watch being set, the King slept on his ship and was met the next morning by King James and his court who sailed the four-mile distance from Greenwich on the royal barge accompanied by at least thirty-five more barges carrying noblemen and dignitaries. The event provided a rare double helping of the spectacle of kingship. The Danish ships themselves were marvellous in their craftsmanship. The King's ship was reckoned to be ten or twelve hundred tons and had three tiers of brass cannons great and small. Her upperworks were richly carved from the beakhead to the poop, much of it gilt with gold leaf. All along the upper decks stood a guard in blue doublets and breeches, white hats, and (it must be said, Malvolio-like) yellow garters. The two kings met and, after a suitable period of on-board entertainment, emerged, whereupon James presented his brother-in-law with a privy barge of his own 'made in the fashion of a Tower, or a little castle, all close with glass windows, and casements fair carved and guilt, and wrought with much art'.[2] The days that followed, according to reports, were filled with hunting and feasting. For the ordinary people in London at the time, the event provided a sumptuous public display of two kings being kings, in other words, a performance of kingship before each other and their respective courts that required the glory of kingship to be unrestrained by mundane encumbrances such as cost.

This is an article about one ordinary man's response to such a spectacle of wealth and power; a response that shows a middle class man's desire to please, to catch the royal eye and thus hope to advance himself; a response that shows the hesitation of a man of limited means at the cost of such a lavish display; and a response that simply shows his awe at the spectacle before him. The response is that of John Davies of Hereford. He was a man of modest background who had distinguished himself well enough in his education to become a tutor at Oxford and a teacher to many of the great families. John Davies was a man from the Marches, those broad, fuzzy borders between England and Wales that, despite their distinctly indistinct qualities, have deep cultural resonance and meaning for those who live in and near them. Indeed, John Davies of Hereford is a man who illustrates many of the practical realities of such borders. Though not a very good poet, he nonetheless showed, in his life as much as in the poem that he wrote to celebrate such a grand state occasion, the realities of what it

---

1 The most descriptive account of the event comes from an anonymously written publication printed by Edward Allde: *The King of Denmarkes welcome: Containing his ariuall, abode, and entertainement, both in the Citie and other places* (1606), 2STC 5194, p. 3. See also H[enry] Roberts, *Englands farevvell to Christian the fourth* (1606), 2STC 21079.

2 *Welcome*, p. 6.

meant to be a man both on and from the borders. Like his place of origin, he was never quite at the centre, always somewhat on the margins. Hereford, his hometown, is even today a border town. Its Welsh name is *Henfford*. Historically, it was a prize for Welsh Kings and a safe garrison from which the English repelled them. Now, it is clearly on the English side, but the question of whether or not Hereford was in the Welsh Marches has itself frequently been unclear. Brian Vickers asserts that in Davies' day the city was in Wales, though all of the early seventeenth-century maps I could find are themselves unclear. This important cathedral city with an indistinct status was not simply Davies's hometown,[3] it was his way of distinguishing himself from his younger, more successful namesake, Sir John Davies, poet and Solicitor General for Ireland under James I. His concern was well placed. Even today, scholars of seventeenth-century poetry blur the two poets together. James Doleman unwittingly conflates the two poets in a discussion of the religious poetry commemorating the accession of King James, and Jonathan Goldberg somewhat amusingly uses the solipsism, 'Sir John Davies of Hereford'.[4]

Davies of Hereford was thus a man who embodied and indeed blurred the margins. He was a man of the rising middle class, an ordinary man in that sense who wanted to better himself. He was a poet, though not one of any great distinction. But he lived near and undoubtedly knew many of the great poets of his day including Shakespeare, Donne, and Mary Herbert, the Countess of Pembroke. He taught members of many of the great families including the Percys, Thomas, Lord Ellesmere, and he almost certainly taught Prince Henry when he was at Oxford. Today, his poetry is largely lost due no doubt to its flat rhymes and his predilection for abstract, ponderous allusions. But, in his defence, his most valuable talent was one that our world of word processors and email no longer has the same value for that it once did: he had beautiful and versatile handwriting. His transcriptions were highly valued in the manuscript culture of the day, and for this talent he achieved no small fame and a tidy income. But it is clear that he sought to be known for his poetry. He published twelve books of poetry between 1602 and 1617. Vickers notes that this was more than either Jonson or Donne, though this is a limited comparison when one accounts for what Ian Donaldson

---

3 Alexander B. Grosart (ed.), 'Memorial Introduction', *The Works of John Davies*, 2 vols. (Edinburgh, 1878), I, ix-lxiii; Charles Driscoll Murphy, 'John Davies of Hereford', PhD thesis, Cornell University, 1940; Mark Eccles, 'Texts and Studies', *Brief Lives: Tudor and Stuart Authors*, special issue of *Studies in Philology*, 79 (1982), pp. 38-9; Brian Vickers, 'John Davies of Hereford: a life of writing', *Shakespeare, A Lover's Complaint, and John Davies of Hereford* (Cambridge: Cambridge University Press, 2007), pp. 15-46.

4 James Doleman, 'The accession of King James I and English religious poetry', *Studies in English Literature*, 34 (1994); or Jonathan Goldberg, *Writing Matter: From the Hands of the English Renaissance* (Stanford, CA: Stanford University Press, 1990), p. 155.

describes as Jonson's 'distaste for the new print medium and for the bookseller's trade'. It is an even more limited comparison in relation to Donne, who kept most of his verse in manuscript and even sought to destroy much of that once he perceived a conflict with his religious vocation.[5] But, it would seem Davies's aspirations as a poet were sensible, if a touch transparent. Poetry in an age of patronage had the potential for profit.

Davies was in the habit of writing poems for the great and the good. He wrote a very long, didactic poem commemorating King James's coronation. *Microcosmos* stretched over 6000 lines touching on a range of topics – nature, the souls of plants and animals, digestion and so on. Regrettably for Davies, the impact of this poem was undoubtedly muted by the fact that James' grand entry into London was delayed by plague. It might also have had something to do with the fact that the tone of his poem could seem somewhat pedantic and its organisation tending to wander, clouding the sense of carefully planned design. Nearly three years on, however, the state visit of Christian IV offered another grand event for Davies's pen.

This meeting of two kings was recorded by a number of prose accounts, all of them fascinated with its sumptuous displays. The two kings' procession through London was especially notable. The Conduits before the Royal Exchange and lower end of Cheapside had been made to run with claret-wine. An artificial arbour had been constructed above the latter 'adorned with fruits of all sortes' including apples, peares, plums, and melons.[6] Further up Cheapside, a large scaffold was constructed where the Recorder of the City and twenty-four Aldermen sat in greeting. Behind them two enormous arches were erected, framing a swath of blue meant to represent the sea and filled with large singing tritons and sea nymphs. Each arch was crowned by two pyramids. Above the left arch Neptune strode a seahorse; above the right, Mulciber, or Vulcan, the god of metals, strode a dragon. The whole scene was further framed by large artificial rocks rising some forty feet high on either side, supported by two Giants. Crowning the tableau were the coats of arms of 'great Bryttain' and Denmark joined together.

Accounts of this pageant failed to clarify how these two coats of arms were joined, whether they were actually joined in a single insignia or merely placed side by side. Davies adopted a higher tone in his poem and made few specific references to the events themselves. There are, however, a few subtle hints that the iconography of the Cheapside pageant guided much of his poem. He referred somewhat obliquely to the arches and the Conduits filled with wine (ll. 65, 298). If that were true, one would be inclined to believe the coats of arms were actually

---

5 Vickers, pp. 23-4; Ian Donaldson, 'Jonson's poetry', *The Cambridge Companion to Ben Jonson*, ed. by Richard Harp and Stanley Stuart (Cambridge: Cambridge University Press, 2000), 119-139.
6 *Welcome*, p. 21.

joined up in some way, for Union and friendship were the themes of the day. 'O Vnion!', shouts Davies, 'that enclaspest in thyne armes, / All that in Heau'n and Earth is great, or good'. Within Davies's ejaculation is the hint of an outline of these joined national symbols. Those arms above the tableau at Cheapside, if the allusion stretches that far, 'enclasped' the things of heaven (like the gods Neptune and Vulcan) and of earth (like the seas). It's difficult to tell from his rather opaque allusiveness, but his repeated use of 'arms' as metaphors for power and political influence as well as for the nations themselves suggest he was imaginatively elaborating on the pageant at Cheapside.

The prose accounts emphasized the displays of warm affection that were exchanged between the two kings and, of course, the Queen: their 'louing and tender imbracements', 'the repetitions of naturall affections' that passed between them.[7] Davies's highest praise was to merge the kings into one. *Bien Venu: Greate Britaines Welcome to Hir Greate Friends, and Deere Brethren The Danes* begins as a prayer. There is no indication that this is meant to be a real prayer, but Davies uses the register of a prayer to the angels to elevate his praise for the two kings to the highest possible level of abstract symbolism:

> Ye Angels which (in Soule inchaunting Quires)
> Do celebrate your Soueraignes holy praise
> Who ever burne in loues refyning fires,
> & concords Tones to highest Thrones do raise
>
> (ll. 1-4)

Abstraction in Davies's poem is, indeed, everywhere. He employs plural nouns for 'Angels', 'fires', 'Tones' and 'Thrones' so one never gets a sense of any specific agent or force. The effect of this rapturous generality is to blur the lines between different modes of distinction, merging the scene into one joyous scene of celebration. This is not just a stylistic quirk (though, to some extent, it is that). It is his poetic strategy for depicting the friendship of these kings, and indeed the kings themselves, in his most complimentary of terms. In many ways both Davies and the other writers recording and celebrating these events were using friendship in a widely accepted Ciceronean tradition popular at that time, a tradition that saw a good friend as a close mirror image of oneself. In *Di Amicitia*, Cicero asserts that 'he who looks upon a true friend, looks, as it were, upon a sort of image of himself'. 'Friendship', he adds, is 'an inclination of the soul joined with a feeling of love rather than from calculation of how much profit the friendship is likely to afford'.[8] It is a pure bond, free of the corruption of competitive self

---

7 Welcome, p. 7.

8 Cicero, *Laelius De Amicitia* (Loeb Classical Library, 1923), sections 7-8, http://penelope.uchicago.edu/Thayer/E/Roman/Texts/Cicero/Laelius_de_Amicitia/text*.html#ref1 (accessed 28 October 2015).

interest. Francis Bacon would express something similar when he stated 'a friend is another himselfe: For that a Friend is farre more than Himselfe'.[9] In his representation of these kings, Davies took these sentiments a step farther. More than a mirror, for him these 'two great Kings so agree[d]', it made one virtually indistinguishable from the other. The Danish King 'Is one with ours', he said, 'to make ours more compleat, / As ours with Him makes Him in better case' (ll.35-36). This state visit was no mere meeting of two sovereigns; it is the moment 'where one King lives in two' (l. 8); sovereignty was one rarefied singular power represented in two bodies. In fact, it was represented thrice over: God, the sovereign of angels, was joyful at the union of these two kings, and this joy was the highest bliss experienced by all who witnessed the sight. Through this divine sovereignty Davies momentarily formed a kind of trinity between God, 'Loves great Lord' (l. 15), and the two kings. He seemed to recall the pageant at Cheapside when he directed his imagined readers to erect 'Arches tryumphall to the Heavens . . . Whereunder threefold-Majestie may pass'. 'Make a Ring', he commanded celestial soldiers, 'About the Kings, wherein your King [God] doth joy: / A twofold Guard make for this twofold King' (ll. 17-19). It was an event that demanded a single response, where the 'joy' of the divine sovereign merges into the 'highest blisse' of everyone (l. 15-16).

Davies was similar in his treatment of the two nations. Again he seemed to sketch the pageant at Cheapside when he ecstatically proclaimed 'Thine Armes those Seas embrace', the two nations' 'Armes, together joyned, can compasse all' (l. 39). But his enthusiasm for this unity was curious given the fact that the British and Danish have frequently found themselves in conflict throughout their history. For this, however, he fondly imagined the period of Danish rule, rhetorically surrendering again 'in love':

> Thou didst of yore (thou worst) command this Land:
> That now againe is present, which is past:
> In Loue, thou maist the Land (inlargd) comand:
> For, it to thee is *So united fast*,
> That one to other cannot choose but stand
> (ll. 42-46)

Union, for Davies though, goes beyond a shared history and royal family. The Danes had a racial similarity too which he admired. 'Looke on the faces of these Danes, our kin', he exclaimed, 'How like they are to us'. They are

> . . . as if we were
> Borne of each other, as we erst have bin;

---

9 Francis Bacon, *The essayes or counsels ciuill* (1639) 2STC 1151, pp. 162.

If likenesse then begets affection deere,
We may exceed in showing (without sinne)
Our Loves to them, as theirs to us appeare
(ll. 169-74)

Davies is clearly fascinated by the spectacle he saw, a display of opulent majesty that filled him with a sense both of awe and purposeful profligacy that attended such occasions, perhaps a bit like contemporary responses to the London, Beijing, and Sochi Olympics. 'Where Kings as one appeare / Uniting so their Raies of Roialty', 'spare no Cost, sith Gold for glori's made, / And glory now is got, which cannot fade' (ll. 124-5, 127-8). His sentiments soon start to run away with him becoming fantastical: 'Get Phænix-feathers' for your crests, tip your launces with diamonds, use rubies for their rests. 'Arme ye in gold' he orders so that Great Britain can be transformed into Peru (ll. 145-52). Yet, here is where we might detect the middle class views of Davies, the ordinary man. Not satisfied with mere praise, Davies is prone to give careful, conservative, even homespun advice. As soon as he praises the glitter and gold of these royal festivities, he pulls back as prudence reigns in his praise. 'Much hurt ensues the interview of Kings' and 'men in strife for Pompe, are divelish Things' (ll. 186, 188). 'Pompe may show her *All*, yet not too much' (l. 120), he cautions. As soon as he exhorts that wine should flow so that 'all may freely drinke', he warns, 'beware of Drunkards fowle designes'. Yet, as if smarting from his own niggardliness and prudishness, Davies spends a good deal of the rest of the poem justifying the expense he has just criticised: 'Though Money be the sinewes of the warres, / It must be spent too, to prevent those Jarres' (ll. 159-60). There is a somewhat touching sense of innocence in Davies's writing. Like all the writers celebrating this event, there is little, if any, irony. His praise and opinions, if a bit too earnest, nonetheless reveal a sense of his own personal investment in this meeting of kings.

There is no doubt that for today's reader, Davies's poetry presents a challenge in its ponderous abstractions and complex syntax. Still, there is evidence that he was read in his own day and that the circle of his readership included the likes of Shakespeare. Brian Vickers has traced one or two probable transformations of Davies's poetry by the bard, and, with that in mind, it is interesting to compare Davies's *Bien Venu* with Shakespeare's own treatment of a meeting of kings written five or six years later. The opening of *Henry VIII* or *All is True* fashions a conversation between the Dukes of Norfolk and Buckingham. They are not 'ordinary men' certainly, but they are nonetheless onlookers to the kings' meeting at the Field of Cloth of Gold. Norfolk's account follows the same structure and strategy as Davies. The kings embrace, and their display of friendship brings a merging of the two men who 'grew together' into 'a compounded one'

79

(1.1.10-12). Lord Buckingham confesses he has been indisposed, a prisoner of his chamber which gives Norfolk the cue to relate what he saw.

> Till this time pomp was single, but now married
> To one above itself. Each following day
> Became the next day's master, till the last
> Made former wonders its. Today the French,
> All clinquant, all in gold, like heathen gods,
> Shone down the English; and, to-morrow, they
> Made Britain India: every man that stood
> Show'd like a mine. Their dwarfish pages were
> As cherubins, all guilt . . .
> (1.1.15-23)[10]

Shakespeare's account, greatly condensed, uses much of the same imagery that Davies did in *Bien Venu*. Where Davies imagined Britain as a new Peru all covered in Gold, Shakespeare transfers a very similar image of otherness to the French who 'clink' in their gold 'like heathen gods'. Even the cherubins correspond in some sense to the Angels of Davies's opening verses. Shakespeare, of course, writes about events in a now distant past and can thus frame the conversation of his characters to imply a greater sense of reservation than Davies could afford. Where we might detect a suppressed flinch at extravagance and expense in Davies's writing, Shakespeare can inject a more knowing, ironical interrogation through Norfolk's account of two kings poised in a cycle of escalating and competitive glamour, each setting new standards for the other with each new day:

> . . . now this masque
> Was cried incomparable; and the ensuing night
> Made it a fool and beggar. The two kings,
> Equal in lustre, were now best, now worst,
> As presence did present them
> (1.1.26-30)

Both Shakespeare and Davies share a sense of the inflationary rhetoric that surrounds these events. Davies is self conscious of his own poetry. He worries that if he has used too many 'Hyperboles', then 'Art should discharge . . . MUCH on loves effect' (ll. 376-7). Shakespeare, as dramatist, is able to stand askance,

---

10 All quotations from Shakespeare are taken from *The Norton Shakespeare*, ed. Stephen Greenblatt, et. al. (New York: WW Norton, 1997).

representing someone very like Davies who struggles to find words rich enough to perform one's appreciation of the royal scene. Shakespeare's Norfolk, like Davies, conflates the two kings:

> ... him in eye,
> Still him in praise: and, being present both
> 'Twas said they saw but one
> (1.1.30-32)

But Norfolk adds a revealing comment on his own observation:

> ... no discerner
> Durst wag his tongue in censure. When these suns –
> For so they phrase 'em – by their heralds challenged
> The noble spirits to arms, they did perform
> Beyond thought's compass
> (1.1.33-36)

'Beyond thought's compass' is a phrase that gives away the strategy that we have been straining to follow. It gives a name to this royal hyperbole that points toward praise beyond our abilities to express in language. Indeed, it draws our attention to the requirement of one performing the inability to give adequate praise: praise beyond praise.

Of course, Christian IV's state visit was not the Field of Cloth of Gold with its hyper competitive, latent aggression underlying every moment. But Shakespeare's parody of royal observers is so well keyed to the tone and strategies used by Davies that one is tempted to wonder if Shakespeare had read his poem to the Danes and had it in mind. Whether or not this is so, the parody frames Davies's conventional sentiments and earnest expression and shows just how limited the language and ambitions of royal praise can be. Davies should have been pleased. Shakespeare goes on to parallel this boundless praise to the financial catastrophe that hit Henry's noblemen. Compelled to spend in support of their King's glorious spectacle, they 'so sickened their estates' that they were never the same again (1.1.81-84). Davies only had his verse in this game, and the end of *Bien Venu* seems to acknowledge the limited options he has in his praise of these kings. The closing thought of this ordinary man's response to such an extraordinary encounter is the modest hope 'That saddest Kings shall read it with delight' (481).

'Henry Vaughan's Grave'
by Christopher Werrett

MARC HARSHMAN

Recoveries

For just this moment, a sweep of swallows conflated
    with a lowering bed of rain-heavy clouds.

A deft toss of hail pebbles against the windows, then silence, then
    comes a blade of sunlight level with the horizon, then it's gone.

Where the stillness sleeps behind the closed door, a shadow
    stretches out as the light goes.

The clock with its tiny feet never quits chasing the moon
    sliding over the cattails and up the mountain into vanishing night.

The morning comes, the skies swift and clear,
    and the ground sodden and glittering
    where the wren whistles its familiar trio of notes.

The creek continues, rushing and urgent in its push
    to join the somewhere seas heedless of time and responsibility.

A wisp of white-yellow larch needles, wind-gathered,
    relax upon the skin of the black water of the ancient swamp.

Thereafter, he swore allegiance to his linen notebook,
    went barefoot, and believed only in the smaller miracles.

Stone

It must have been last night the moon threw down this stone, or the earth
    let it float loose, up, and returned it to light.
A stone as silent as a new-dug grave.
A stone with a history longer than even the endless cycling
    of the little stream here behind me racing a nameless forest to the sea.

Imagine how long the things of this earth must sometimes wait to be heard.
And yet this stone squats upon this green turf in its snug
    and impermeable white skin,
    as patient as a fox in the lap of the Buddha,
    while the thin noon of March slowly lifts over our tawdry certainties.

Nearby cardinals are warming up their spring song,
    tossing it between the branches of a slender hemlock.
They are the apples of winter.
They are bright-feathered engines of blood and wonder.
They are here to speak,
    to re-member the sentience of all things.
All I have to do is translate. I don't have to worry
    about getting it right. Eternity is for that, and this day
    I only plan to look over its gates, part the lower branches,
    squint, listen to what whispers, cradle this stone in the palm of my hand
    and speak with it as if it were resilient metaphor
    willing to accept my give and take,
    as capable of every term in life's taxonomy as I am.

I am tossing it back and forth between my left and my right hand.
And now, right now, I am tossing it to you, and will wait
    for you to toss it back with your own understanding
    that this moment has been,
    as we might some day be ourselves,
    silent, small, and
    perfect as a stone, patient,
    and listening,
    as I am
    for what comes next.

GRAHAM HARTILL

for Anne

'Since death alone is certain
and the time of death uncertain,
what should I do?

*

Wake at 6 in the morning
with the fact
that the moment of life-and–death
is upon us

Wake up!

She presented the gleaming animal world
to us all
who stumble in the field of harm

Migrating Bones

But aren't they always?

and isn't this
the oldest thing

the dead being wild,
being out of control?

the spirits
heading
back to the woods?

*

that forestry beyond the ridge,
Coed Du,
before they felled it –

one winter day I wouldn't go in,
so dark
and thick with snow –
a vast heavy roof
and the thinnest light
in the avenues

or that dream, in the early 80's,
of ashes
whispering down the chimney –

only that –

I woke afraid –

went the long way round instead
trudging through fields of dazzling snow

Edward Thomas
left a feather of presence,
a sign
for anyone to follow

yet, if we do follow
must it be all the way
to the suicide of war
(war being suicide by other means),

not just into one's unconscious
but the *world's* unconscious,
an *unfathomable*
depression?

that won't do, of course –
even calling it such,
just calling it,
reels it in
and makes it comprehensible,
manageable,
language bringing the open world
into being,
meaning
negotiation
with open light

and any agreement dependent on us
using of course
the same currency:
Trust –

no, not just the unconscious
but an unconscious beyond the unconscious,
the *wild*,
the fangs!
the eyes of the dog in full chase
its major joy,
the exuberance of its life

being what terror is for –
it's fight or flight

and my own terrors?
drowning,
the fear of being out of reach
of my own interior mother?

half-way through Dante's Wood,
or call it
Wilfred Owen's profound dull tunnel,
Eliot's London Bridge,
Hansel and Gretel's European forest,

or that prisoner's story that haunts me
of looking from Chiron's boat at all the houses we have built in life
in tumbling ruins
(shall we say like Babel?) –

all you have made in life
pulled down –
it is war,
the ruins of deserted cities,
the post-industrial coming to nothing
I grew up with,
out of

*

and it is finally
the mystery
of our bodies,

the brain
the darkest and most complex forest –

and what shall
I leave behind me?

a new
feather?

Edward Thomas: The Green Roads
Anne Cluysenaar: Shetland Ewe, in Migrations

ROSIE JACKSON

Mary Shelley, Hyde Park, 1850

She tries to avoid the Serpentine, but today
it's on her before she's aware: a mouth that doesn't close,
green water pulling her.

Not that she cares for reflections any more,
her hair grown thin, the skin on her face slack,
as if carelessly stitched.

Always fighting to keep the membrane intact,
to stop the dead pushing through,
not see her baby in these carriages in the park,

not remember the feel of her husband's collarbone
inside his open-necked shirt,
the drum of his heart under naked ribs.

But now her hand has reached into the lake,
found Harriet as she lies there,
drifting under the surface like pondweed.

And when Harriet's fingers stick to hers,
she doesn't prise them away, but nods: *Yes,*
I was the one who stole your young husband,

I was the one who stole lightning from the gods
and made a man. And they took away my marriage,
its angels of rain and light, and child after child in return.

The trees are white, everything in London white.
The pavement, turned to ice, cracks underfoot
and bodies lie in the ocean beneath her; ropes; oars; tiny bones.

She pulls up her collar. *How tame I have become,*
shrinking from the west wind. Is this what grief has done?
Left me on the side of shadows? And when she sits to write,

the words are snow and cannot warm her,
even her quiet moments too full of apocalypse.
This is how it is when the world has no mother.

John Donne Arriving in Heaven

He knew it would be a melting, looking back
at the world as a place of icicles and clouds,
lilies of passion unmooring their tangled roots.

Knew that with the rungs of prayer and reason
knocked away, the subtle knot undone,
he would step into this delicate permanence,

the light cleansing, as protracted evening sun
perfects a field of harvest corn.
Expected such radiance that finds no flaws

in all that's happened, no severity,
only the mercy of a paradise always autumn,
its joy possessed, ripe, perfect, complete.

But this is less the arrival he foresaw
than an undoing of distances, a shedding
of himself to become who he already was,

not gaining union but losing the illusion
he was separate, was ever other than this one:
the hand that set all things in motion,

spread this equal light, made on a whim
the stars, the schoolboys, the unruly sun.
All love a dream of this. And now, as he takes on

the bliss, the infinite bliss his little deaths
on earth struggled to reach, he finds his words
at last translated to their proper tongue.

'Vaughan Variations': Anne Cluysenaar in conversation with Henry Vaughan

JEREMY HOOKER

Internal evidence shows that Anne Cluysenaar's 'Vaughan Variations'[1] were written in the early to mid-1990s during the period of the Bosnian war. She was intensely aware of the suffering caused by the siege of Sarajevo and throughout the murderous conflict. War was partly what drew her to Henry Vaughan, poet of another civil war, in which he had fought in a losing cause, and from which he had suffered. Vaughan, alive in his poetry for Cluysenaar, was a neighbour from across the Usk Valley, though separated by more than three hundred years. The poets had in common a landscape, changed but with lasting features. They were close in their needs, despite being separated by time, with all that it implies of historical and cultural differences. Closeness and distance, affinity and differences, within the shared Brecheiniog landscape, describe what 'Vaughan Variations' are about.

The poems are intensely personal. They contain elements of autobiography, some of it dealing with difficult matters which the poet is experiencing or remembering as she writes. They also touch upon intimate aspects of Henry Vaughan's life, so that in reading them Vaughan the poet becomes for the reader a complex, living man. The poems are concerned with healing, Cluysenaar's felt need, which draws her to the doctor poet's and his alchemist brother's healing arts. She is both seeking Vaughan out, as we see in the first 'Variation', and coming to him as a seeker after wholeness. Underlying all the themes, 'Vaughan Variations' is a conversation about poetry, in which the modern poet makes discoveries about her art in the process of writing, and through interpreting the art of the seventeenth-century metaphysical poet. Vaughan emerges from the conversation as in some ways modern, and at the same time part of an ancient poetic tradition, which is still alive in the late 20th century.

---

1 'Vaughan Variations' is a sequence of 23 poems, which forms part of Anne Cluysenaar's *Timeslips:* New and Selected Poems , Carcanet, 1997. Quotations from the sequence and from all Cluysenaar's poems will be from this edition, referenced *T* in the text.

The epigraph to the sequence as a whole is from Henry Vaughan's 'Love-Sick':

> . . . make these mountains flow,
> These mountains of cold ice in me.[2]

The epigraph to 'Variation' 1 is from 'Affliction' (1):

> . . . that's best
> Which is not fixed, but flies and flows . . . (R, p. 219)

The lines from 'Love-Sick' connect inner and outer landscapes: 'mountains of cold ice in me'. They indicate emotional crisis, something frozen in the poet who has chosen them, which she wishes to release. There is crisis in the poet's life and in her time, as there was in Henry Vaughan's. The need in both poets is for liberating emotional growth.

The quotation from 'Affliction' (1) repeats the word 'flow'. This is a key concept for 'Vaughan Variations' and indeed for Cluysenaar's poetry generally. In 'Affliction' (1) Henry Vaughan emphasizes the divine necessity of 'vicissitude', the order in which man's physic or medicine is futile compared to God's 'great elixir', 'a sacred, needful art' that is the transformative power ordering the whole creation. For Anne Cluysenaar, this power exists in nature and the self, and in the healing that Henry Vaughan, as poet and doctor, represents.

The emphasis upon flowing underlines the importance for Cluysenaar of natural processes. This is a theme which she develops through the poems in 'Timeslips'[3] and in 'Vaughan Variations' and subsequent work. In 'Timeslips' and other, earlier poems, we see a poet who is tough-minded, scientifically informed, and sensitive, an existential explorer of what it means to be human in a world that has evolved and is evolving. She is a poet aware of the centrality of language to human consciousness, and of the part evolution plays in language. In consequence, she is acutely sensitive to the creativity of 'matter':

> With which we make, of which we are made.
> Ancient and new, unpredictably changing.
> It strikes through the robin's wing,
> through the pruned rose, through the stare
> of the dog, the thrust
> of the weed, from a heap of domestic dust.
> Day things. Among them, familiar, the human word.
> ('Vaughan Variations' 15, T, p. 148)

---

2 *Henry Vaughan: The Complete Poems*, ed. Alan Rudrum, Penguin Classics, 1983, p. 257. Further Vaughan quotations will be from this edition, referenced R in the text.

3 'Timeslips' is a section of poems within the book of that title.

Her poetry gives powerful expression to time as the medium of continuous creativity, linking the living with the dead. Thus, in 'About the Church', a poem preceding 'Timeslips', she describes a graveyard as 'a place . . . cut across fibres / of continuous time'.

> Follow any one
> tombstone, it will lead through ancestral crowds
> into millions – beyond civilised man, and Man,
> to wordless creatures, down to the persistent

> minute beings whose efforts created us. (*T*, p. 76)

From wordless creatures to Man, the word-user, life is a process of creative effort. Water imagery, drawn especially from the Gwent coast and the river Usk, expressive of the creative process, flows through Cluysenaar's poetry. So also does imagery of light and shadow. This forms a strong connection with the Vaughan twins, who 'developed a fascination with water and light'.[4]

The concern with process in 'Vaughan Variations' is psychological as well as evolutionary and geological. In this respect, it relates to the poet's vulnerability as she searches for a personal centre. This connects her to writers in the seventeenth century, as Stevie Davies describes them:

> The problem of constructing a viable 'self' in an age of controversy, civil turmoil and scepticism was shared in common with many contemporaries. 'Our selves,' confessed Donne, are 'What we know not'. Montaigne had pointed out and Donne agreed, that the self is a process, changing and in flow like a river . . . The miasma of ontological uncertainty in a period of scepticism affected many thinking people . . .[5]

So it does in our time, and 'Vaughan Variations' gives it notable expression in the life of one woman, her self 'a process, changing and in flow like a river'.

Self as process is a determining factor in the composition of 'Vaughan Variations', and Cluysenaar sees it playing a similar role in Vaughan's poems. In 'Distraction', for example, she perceives 'a molten flow in which words and experience come simultaneously, both provisional and both, for that very reason, vibrantly alive'.[6] Style thus becomes a mode of exploration, as in Wallace Stevens, for Cluysenaar the supremely important modern poet. According to her, 'Distrac-

---

4 Anne Cluysenaar, Introduction, *Henry Vaughan: Selected Poems*, The Golden Age of Spiritual Writing, SPCK, 2004, p. 1.

5 Stevie Davies, *Henry Vaughan*, The Border Lines Series, Seren, 1995, p. 75.

6 Anne Cluysenaar, "Rereading Henry Vaughan's 'Distraction'", *Scintilla* 1, 1997, p. 94.

tion' is the kind of poem Stevens wrote, and which he described as 'the poem of the mind in the act of finding / What will suffice'. As it continues, the quotation from 'Of Modern Poetry' applies to 'Vaughan Variations' as a whole: 'Its past was a souvenir. It has to be living . . . It has to face the time . . . It has to think about war / And it has to find what will suffice'.

'Vaughan Variations' 1 enters at once into a landscape Cluysenaar shares with Vaughan. The Brecheiniog landscape of the poets is a place of

> falling water between mountains
> whose high heads throw moving shadows
> to tell time, emptying the fields. (*T*, p. 129)

It is a temporal landscape and a place of flowing rhythms and of light and shadow. Cluysenaar depicts a landscape of transformative energies, in which place and language are inter-connected:

> At other times, I've looked for you
> in your language, shapes that you'd own
> traced by words that change and die off. (*T*, p. 129)

'Shapes' refer to both land and poems – poems through which land is known. Language changes, but it carries meaning through; it communicates across time; it transmits. This inter-personal, communicative, transmissive character of language is Cluysenaar's principal concern as poet and linguist. Literally placing the Vaughan twins in or by the river Usk, she sees how their language develops in relation to place:

> I see here how your voice and his
> might evolve their ways. Toddler-talk
> of twins, down by that clear amber,
> half drowned in its hushed and hushing,
> the soft pour pf those melting pleats –
> made and remade, same shapings in
> changing water. Your mother's tongue,
> then English, making, remaking.
> Swirled by what can't be said. (*T*, p. 129)

Her focus here is upon language's creativity, the part it plays in evolving identity: its making and remaking, and also the pressure upon it of 'what can't be said'. Her awareness of the relation between language and reality is modern, scientific (with a particular debt to Erwin Schrödinger),[7] and again owes a debt to Stevens concerning imagination as world-making. The water metaphor places the Vaughan boys in language, as they are in the river. And language is 'Swirled by what can't be said' – words that suggest the unsayable mystery is nevertheless an energy perceivable through words. Her religious sense does not have the structure of Henry Vaughan's religious belief, but it comes through strongly in 'Vaughan Variations', where it acquires some definition.

Language, as Cluysenaar understands it, 'has made you too real, / like a parent after his death' (*T*, p. 129). Her relationship with Henry Vaughan has been described as a love affair.[8] He might also be described as her father figure. Both descriptions point to the emotional intensity of the relationship. It is love that recognises difference, together with what cannot be known. It honours Henry Vaughan's otherness. And it releases feeling for people in Anne Cluysenaar's life, especially her parents.

The epigraph to 'Vaughan Variations' 2 is from Vaughan's 'The True Christmas', a distressed, angry poem, with what may be described as a puritan spirit.

> The brightness of this day we owe
> Not unto *music, masque* nor *show*:
> Nor gallant furniture, nor plate;
> But to the manger's mean estate. (*R*, p. 374)

Cluysenaar's poem connects the Christ-child born in a manger to 'the baby girl' injured by a shell in Sarajevo. The contemporary wounding and killing brings Vaughan to mind:

> I seem to see you, poet
> who had fought in a civil war,
> doctor on edge with winter deaths,
> taking your pen at Christmas time –
> impatient, starting a poem
> 'So stick up ivy . . .' (*T*, 131)

The quotation sounds like a curse. 'I seem to see you' is tactful, acknowledging Vaughan the stranger. The following verse paragraph begins: 'No way of foreseeing us'. Vaughan exists in his time. But the poem disrupts time's confinement:

---

7 For Cluysenaar's discussion of the modern model of 'reality' and its debt to scientific thinking, in which she refers to Schrödinger's *Mind and Matter*, see her essay, 'Post-culture: Pre-culture?', in *British Poetry Since 1960*, eds. Michael Schmidt and Grevel Lindop, Carcanet, 1972, pp. 215-232.

8 Personal communication from Gwyneth Lewis.

> May he discover, as he rides,
> the clean grey branches of the ash
> preparing their black buds, and in
> a sheltered covert those hanging
> dashes of hazel, loosening,
> as they do now. Something we can't
> stop, or bring on. Not metaphors. (*T*, p. 131)

What the verse makes us accept is astonishing. Here, Vaughan is alive, a man with a future: 'May he discover . . .' It is nature that enables this sense of continuity; and it is language.

In subtle ways, Cluysenaar conducts a conversation with Vaughan in time and across time: a conversation with one speaker, which is not a monologue. Vaughan is a presence; he speaks through his poems, and he speaks to the poet in her need. Cluysenaar has faith in language's power to communicate between individuals and to transmit across time. Her strongest prose statement of this occurs in 'To the Reader' which prefaces *Double Helix*, the book combining her mother's memoirs with her poems in response:

> as I read her memoirs I became possessed by astonishment at the way a simple language of natural signs can survive the changing generations and acquire meanings which everyday language seldom embodies. I think that 'poetry' has its root in such signs. In all the individuality of its cultural incarnations, it represents something shared by all human beings.[9]

This faith in language is faith in a poem's capacity to be 'a metaphor for the way universal experiences come to us through, not in spite of, individual responses and thoughts'.[10] Cluysenaar's poetry deploys 'natural signs', from the miniscule to the astronomical, and is rich in particularity. In the passage quoted above, 'clean grey branches of the ash / preparing their black buds', and 'those hanging dashes / of hazel', speak a language Henry Vaughan knew, and knew by bodily touch, as his natural signs speak to us. Cluysenaar's later work, *Touching Distances*,[11] further develops this art of intimate connection between individuals and across time.

Cluysenaar has 'no prayers for the dead / or the living' (*T*, p. 130). She does not share Vaughan's Christian faith. But her poems have a numinous quality analogous to Vaughan's – a quality perceived in the landscape of river and moun-

---

9 Anne Cluysenaar and Sybil Hewat, *Double Helix*, Carcanet and Mid Northumberland Arts Group,, 1982, p. 9.
10 Ibid., p. 9.
11 Anne Cluysenaar, *Touching Distances*: Diary Poems, Cinnamon Press, 2013.

tains, in light and shadow, in natural patterns and rhythms, in trees and flowers and creatures – in a word, in *quickness*.[12] They show an attentiveness that found expression in a religious form later, when she joined the Quakers. Her special affinity is with Vaughan as a 'green' poet, as he has come to be seen by other poets and readers in recent years.

Henry Vaughan is present in 'Vaughan Variations' but not in a sentimental way that abolishes distance or reduces his otherness. 'Vaughan Variations' 3 begins:

> I invented it, so why
> since then, do I see your hand
> come of its own accord to the mind's eye? (*T*, p. 132)

She recognises her vision of Vaughan's writing hand as a 'trespass', an illegitimate crossing from where she is to 'where-you-were'. With this comes realization that: 'This is the space, then, / imagination would have me know. / The space that tastes of self'. The time is dawn, the numinous hour Vaughan loved. In this shared hour, Cluysenaar writes with vulnerable intimacy, which combines frankness and directness with a haunting sense of the numinous:

> No candle now in the grey dawn
> but a bulb. It's at this hour
> your heart's events, genesis, restoration,
> come, though in new terms, nearer.
> How I need your frankness here!
> A stuttering permission
> (though all the *but's* crowd in) to praise.
> Standing at the window, I hear you say
> quietly, 'Mornings are mysteries.'
> Despite the disgraces that mark our century,
> still the page calls for difficult honesties.
> And would pass them on, from here to there. (*T*, p. 132)

Cluysenaar, a modern poet, finds in Vaughan 'a stuttering permission / . . . to praise'. She hears his voice: 'Mornings are mysteries'. Her mind has gone to his poem, 'Rules and Lessons', which is at once a sermon and a hymn of praise:

> Walk with thy fellow-creatures: note the *hush*
> And whispers amongst them. There's not a *spring*,

---

12 The reference here is to Vaughan's poem 'Quickness' and especially its concluding lines: 'But life is, what none can express/ *A quickness, which my God hath kissed*', *R*, p. 308.

> Or *leaf* but hath his *morning-hymn*; each *bush*
> And *oak* doth know I AM; cans't thou not sing? (*R*, p. 193)

She can sing, but not like this. What she receives from Vaughan – 'heart's events, genesis, restoration' – comes through 'in new terms'. If the terms were not new there would be no new poetry, no 'Vaughan Variations', and no transmission from Henry Vaughan to Anne Cluysenaar and from her to us. What he passes to her, and she wishes to pass on, includes 'difficult honesties'.

These are personal. They concern the poet's emotions, her sense of self, her response to 'the disgraces that mark our century', and her relationships. Primary among the latter are her relationships with her parents. 'Vaughan Variations' 9 concerns her father; 'Vaughan Variations' 22 remembers her mother. Both are about creativity. The latter is a wonderfully sensuous rendering of making apple puree, with the poet doing the work and remembering her mother doing it. The epigraph from Vaughan's 'The Match' – 'Settle my *house*, and shut out all distractions / That may unknit / My heart . . .' (*R*, p. 192) – relates to the mother as centre of order in the house. The poem includes the poignant lines:

> Now that
> I do the work, it's different:
> no child will imagine me
> the centre of her world. (*T*, p. 158)

Cluysenaar had no child of her own. This fact intensified her conviction about transmission, and her desire to pass her poetry on, 'from here to there'.[13]

'Vaughan Variation' 9, written *'In the ninth year since my father's burial'*, challenges interpretation. This may be because of 'difficult honesties', or because of the Belgian painter's struggles with his art. Its epigraph is from Vaughan's 'The Holy Communion': 'Nothing that is, or lives, / But hath his quickenings, and reprieves' (*R*, p. 217). Vaughan's poem is about God the life-giver. The darkness at Jesus' death gave us sight: 'Did make us see / The way to thee'. Jesus paid a terrible price to enable us to see.

Cluysenaar's poem begins with the burial of her father in a Belgian graveyard. It is compacted with imagery of constriction, which suggests also the painter's abstract canvases:

> Just a box-hedge emblem,
> evergreen, marking off the hectare, denial

---

13 I call here upon conversations with the poet.

of what the countryside flamed with – stubble
stretching all round the churchless graveyard.
A dark oblong, a bowless barge, a hard
stillness on that swell of bright lines closing
toward flat horizons on every side. (*T*, p. 138)

As in 'barge' and 'swell', sea imagery runs through descriptions of the landscape
and the painter's abstract art. This suggests a rebuke to 'denial' of energy, and
a desire for more, something wilder, a depth beyond. As I understand it, this
symbolises what the artist desired. It certainly intimates what his daughter seeks
in her poetry, as she reflects in response to her father's question:

'*Comment ferias-tu ça en poesie*'
me demandait-il, of some technical trick
that was always more – a formal magic
not against but beyond thought, like music
or the way words work with silence in poetry. (*T*, p. 139)

For the poet, 'some technical trick . . . was always more – a formal magic'.
    Magic is a vital force in 'Vaughan Variations'. The word should remind us that
the sequence is also about Thomas Vaughan, the alchemist, with whom his twin
brother, Henry, shared so much. Alchemy is both a subject of the sequence and
an influence upon its imagery. In 'Vaughan Variations' 8 Cluysenaar sees the
twins in 'two noisy lads' playing 'under Tal-y-Bont's wild waterfall':

Each feels a ring round his chest, like
the mouth of a fish, the scales flashing
to fire under his beating palms.
From the ledge above, new water comes,
a cold breath of white sound falling.
But where they are, it's *igne tincta,*
water 'tinged with fire'. Origins. (*T*, p. 137)

The lads she sees call to mind the Vaughan twins. The reference to "*igne tincta,* /
water 'tinged with fire'" transports us into the heart of the alchemist's imaginative world. In her Introduction to her selection of Henry Vaughan's poems
Cluysenaar quotes Thomas Vaughan's *Euphrates, Or the Waters of the East*, in
which he speaks of his childhood fascination with 'the continual action of fire
upon water'.[14] In Preface to *The Fame & Confession* Thomas Vaughan describes

14 Introduction, *Henry Vaughan: Selected Poems*, p. 1.

Aqua Igne tinctus as: 'in the *Center* of every *thing* there was a perfect *Unity*, a miraculous indissoluble *Concord* of *Fire* and *Water*'.[15] The concordance of opposites informs a metaphysical tradition in English poetry, which connects the Vaughans with Blake and Coleridge and certain modern poets. Its appearance in 'Vaughan Variations' 8 is doubly significant. First, the poet perceives the image central to the imagination – "*igne tincta*, / water 'tinged with fire' – in an everyday scene recalling the Vaughan boys' initiation in mystery. It is here, in our world, that the magic occurs. Secondly, the visionary moment raises what is perhaps the most important question for Cluysenaar in 'Vaughan Variations':

> What, in this century, can be made
> in language, not to deny this? (*T*, p. 138)

The question is about 'Origins' – specifically, about the origins of the metaphysical imagination, and therefore, by implication, about poetry in our time.

Henry Vaughan was a visionary poet, but one who suffered for his visions. Anne Cluysenaar sees him as a man of his time, one who struggled to achieve wholeness. As she says in 'Vaughan Variations' 11:

> He didn't deny them, the contradictions,
> the twists of mind and mood, the boring
> *et ceteras*, the grit between visions,
> and the visions themselves, unaccountable,
> unearned, hard to own up to.
> Because of war, imperfection, change.
>
> He would work, to heal himself
> and others, with words or herbs. (*T*, p. 142)

Nothing was easy for Vaughan. That is why he speaks to a poet with her own struggles, in a time darkened by war and other disgraces. It was through his struggles that he became a poet with a healing vision. A question implied at the heart of 'Vaughan Variations' is whether this is possible for a poet towards the end of the twentieth century. For us, it also raises the question of what kind of poet Anne Cluysenaar was.

An essay she wrote about poetry in the 1960s helps to place her in relation to her contemporaries. In it, we see how her profession as a linguist coincided

---

15 *The Works of Thomas Vaughan*, ed. Alan Rudrum, with the Assistance of Jennifer Drake-Brockman, Clarendon Press, Oxford, 1984, p. 510.

with the instincts that drove her poetry. In *Introduction to Literary Stylistics*, she wrote:

> as linguists have pointed out, language is of more than immediate personal, or indeed public, importance to man, since it is the vehicle of 'non-biological heredity', the vehicle (that is) of our contacts with the past and the future as well as the present.[16]

While showing herself fully alive to the intellectual and cultural crisis of the modern age, exacerbated by the war and use of the A-bomb, she retains her conviction that language connects the present to past and future. This influences her assessment of other poets. Thus, while respectful, her discussion of the dominant English poets of the time, Sylvia Plath and Ted Hughes, recognises their limitations. In the context of discussing Plath she says:

> There is perhaps something in the thought that the worse and more direct the experience, the more right one may feel one has, if one recovers, to take horror for granted and to construct something positive – to feel that the dead impose a duty to live rather than a duty to mourn.[17]

She quotes James Burns Singer's 'The Gentle Engineer'. 'I carry that which I am carried by', and contrasts Singer's stance with Hughes's: "This sense of being part of the universe, not lost in it, allows for a more positive formulation than does 'wodwoism'".[18] The impression of Hughes's 'Wodwo' and 'Crow' is 'of a creature dissociated from its environment'.

Singer's poetry, informed by his profession as a scientist, was important to Cluysenaar. She would later edit and introduce a selection of his poems.[19] In this essay, she makes a creedal statement linking Singer and Wallace Stevens, and quotes words from Stevens that she makes her own:

> Singer's sense of himself, of man, as a part of reality – as reality become conscious, able to speak of itself – is a radically different conception from that of a creature in a hostile world into which it has somehow been dropped. Our minds may, by long habit, seem to us to be 'over against' reality but in fact they are certainly part of it. *I am a part of what is real, and that is my speech, and the strength of it, this only, that I hear*

---

16 Anne Cluysenaar, *Introduction to Literary Stylistics*, B. T. Batsford, 1976, p. 26.
17 'Post-Culture: Pre-Culture?', *British Poetry Since 1960*, p. 221.
18 Ibid, p. 224.
19 *Burns Singer: Selected Poems*, ed. Anne Cluysenaar, Carcanet, 1977.

and ever shall. Man is a means for the forces he wishes to understand to understand themselves.[20]

Some years after writing this essay Anne Cluysenaar would move to Wales, to a smallholding on the edge of Wentwood Forest and close to Henry Vaughan's native ground across the Usk Valley. One may ask, therefore, what influence living in Wales had on her determination 'to construct something positive', as a woman who believed she was 'a part of what is real'. In attempting to answer this question one should begin by saying that it did not change her essentially – she had been a poet with a positive attitude since childhood, and there are continuities in all her published work. Life in Wales did, however, give her new subject matter and new confidence as a poet, and enhanced her ability to express her sense of being part of reality. This sense was at once instinctive and a conviction of the relationship between language and reality. Her encounter with Henry Vaughan's poetry, in the landscape in which it had been written, was crucial. And in his poetry she found an exploratory art that took her deeper into Welsh culture.

Cluysenaar approached Vaughan's 'unfeigned verse'[21] as a linguist and a reader and practitioner of modern exploratory poetry, such as Wallace Stevens. She appreciated Vaughan's 'organic' forms: the poem as thinking-in-process. Taking issue with Jonathan Post's view of 'Distraction' as 'disorganized', she says: the poem "can so easily be experienced as a series of 'contour-following rings . . . with hidden ways'".[22] The reference is to Gwyn Williams's Foreword to *The Burning Tree,* which confirmed her suspicion that Vaughan had been influenced by Welsh poetry. Williams contrasts the 'centred design', which 'English and most Western European creative activity' inherited 'from Greece and Rome', with the different, 'specific view of composition' of Welsh poetry. The Welsh poets, Williams says, 'were not trying to write poems that would read like Greek temples or even Gothic cathedrals but, rather, like stone circles or the contour-following rings of the forts from which they fought, with hidden ways slipping from one ring to another'. He claims 'that this idea of composition is still potent' in the twentieth century, and, by implication, in English-language poetry, as demonstrated by Dylan Thomas and David Jones.[23]

This view of poetic composition links Welsh verse to the physical and historical landscape of Wales. For Cluysenaar, it provided an evocative metaphor for

---

20 Ibid., p. 231. The words in italics adapt, and make personal to Cluysenaar, a passage from Stevens's *The Necessary Angel.* She places the quotation at the head of her essay, where she says: 'These words may very well be an inscription above the portal of what lies ahead'.
21 Henry Vaughan, 'Anguish', *R,* p. 294.
22 "Rereading Henry Vaughan's 'Distraction'", *Scintilla* 1, 105.
23 Gwyn Williams, Foreword, *The Burning Tree,* Faber, 1956, p. 15.

the Gwent in which she had settled, and a description of the writing process –
the organic form – she shared with Henry Vaughan.

Vaughan as a Welsh poet is most bardic in the letter about the Bards that he
sent to John Aubrey. In this, he records a story he has been told of a poor young
man who 'was taken up by a rich man, that kept a great stock of sheep upon
the mountains not far from the place where I now dwell'. The young man falls
asleep and has a dream:

> he saw a beautifull young man with a garland of green leafs upon his
> head, & a hawk upon his fist; with a quiver full of Arrows att his back,
> coming towards him (whistling several measures or tunes all the way) &
> at last lett the hawk fly at him, wch (he dreamt) gott into his mouth &
> inward parts, & suddenly awaked in a great fear & consternation: but
> possessed with such a vein, or gift of poetrie, that he left the sheep & went
> about the Countrey, making songs upon all occasions, and came to be
> the most famous Bard in all the Countrey in his time. (*T*, pp. 143-144)

It is fascinating to hear this story from the lips of a sophisticated gentleman
such as Henry Vaughan, and one may wonder what exactly it meant to him.
Certainly it had roots in his childhood when he and his brother heard from
their teacher, Matthew Herbert, 'In dark records and numbers nobly high / The
visions of our black, but brightest bard'.[24] The inspirational figure described in
the letter descends from such 'visions', from stories of Myrddin and Orpheus,
and has affinities with that spirit of nature, the Green Man. Significantly, the
story occurred 'upon the mountains not far from the place where I now dwell'.
It is a local story, with roots deep in myth and ancient poetic tradition.

Cluysenaar makes the letter 'the centre-piece' of 'Vaughan Variations', and
thus emphasises her sense of Vaughan as a 'green' poet and a poet with, at least,
a bardic strain. This is a healing role with implications for Vaughan as a shamanic
figure: one who, 'following his or her experience of personal disintegration, seeks
to become a bridge for others between the material world and the world of the
spirit'.[25] Henry Vaughan was such 'a bridge' for Anne Cluysenaar.

But what do we mean by calling poems in 'Vaughan Variations' numinous:
'bridges' 'between the material world and the world of the spirit'? The tenth
poem in the sequence has an epigraph from 'Midnight':

> What emanations
> Quick vibrations
> And bright stirs are there? (*R*, p. 175)

---

24 'Daphnis: An Elegiac Eclogue', *R*, p. 387.
25 Introduction, *Henry Vaughan: Selected Poems*, p. 6.

In 'Midnight', Vaughan, as he often does, is watching 'Thy heavens', which '(some say) / Are a firy-liquid light'. He pleads with God to 'Shine in this blood, / And water in one beam',

> And thou shalt see
> Kindled by thee
> Both liquors burn, and stream,
>   O what bright quickness,
>   Active brightness,
> And celestial flows
>   Will follow after
>   On that water,
> Which thy spirit blows! (*R*, p. 175)

All the images central to Vaughan's religious vision coalesce here. 'Quickness' ('life is, what none can express, / *A quickness, which my God hath kist*'); starlight; fire in water: *Aqua Igne Tinctus*, 'a perfect unity, in the *Center* of everything'. The foundation of this is biblical: 'he that cometh after me . . . shall baptize you with the Holy Ghost, and with fire' (Matthew 3. 11). What Vaughan with his imagination sees in the universe is Christian alchemy, which is dynamic and life-giving. Stevie Davies describes this well:

> Nothing in the universe of Vaughan's poetry is insentient. Spirit flows boundlessly through all creation, pouring back the Divine love to its source.[26]

In 'Vaughan Variations' 10, Cluysenaar perceives her numinous vision in landscape and light:

> The hills from this height,
> and the valley, look shadowless,
> as if light from within
> had replaced the sun. (*T*, 140)

Initially the dematerialising effect is a release from bodily limitation. Drawing her imagery from physics and optics, she writes:

> It seems. It seems
> a rolling meniscus,

---

26 *Henry Vaughan*, p. 14.

holding only just.
Pressed between different
densities. Fragile
immense location.

Awareness of the universe as 'immense location' comes as it is broken, returning the poet to her specific place:

The thin circle
of grass-blade and shadow
on a stone by my head
trembles a little.

Nothing to be afraid of.
I can smell the warm
ewe's wool as a lamb
butts and suckles.
For me too
a place waits
in which love can be
natural as death. (*T*, pp. 140 – 141)

Here, she acknowledges, 'formula and word / both fail'. But natural signs do not, and it is in imagery of birth and sustaining, protective love (ewe and lamb) that she finds means to express her faith in 'a place . . . / in which love can be / natural as death'. Cluysenaar ends the poem by asking how Vaughan could believe in 'an orphan lad' receiving from 'a youth / garlanded in green' gifts of 'fear and poetry'. The poem thus points forward to the centre of 'Vaughan Variations' and the natural magic of the story of the 'green' poet. It reminds us that love and poetry, together with fear, including a sense of awe, are what the sequence is about.

In 'Vaughan Variations' 23 the poet says:

These days, in the valley, the steady bell,
when it steps our way, brings few of us back.
Some literalists. Some hearers of metaphor. (*T*, p. 161)

The bell is that of the church which has replaced the one in which Henry and Thomas Vaughan worshipped, the building, representative of the world, 'full of *Spirit, quick,* and *living*.[27] Cluysenaar does not pretend to be intimate with Vaughan's religious faith. She approaches him through language, through metaphor, and through a shared love of nature; she does not speak of God. What she has made in 'Vaughan Variations' is, nevertheless, 'full of Spirit, quick, and living'.

The word 'conversation' suggests at least two speakers. 'Vaughan Variations' is the work of one poet; but it is not a monologue. For Cluysenaar, Vaughan is alive in his poetry, in what she calls, in 'Vaughan Variations' 5, 'his mind's movements', and in the shared place. In 'Vaughan Variations' 18 she holds a stone that Vaughan may have held, a stone made through ages of geological time. It is an emblem of transmission between both poets and beyond them. The contact is a kind of touch that words and things mediate:

> Your poems remember you
> by the spring here, or on the ridge
> with Llangorse Lake exhaling
> its milky dreams or drawing
> to itself an elixir of dew,
> day slowly cooling. (*T*, p. 152)

Memory of the poems imbues the place with magic: 'an elixir of dew'. In this landscape, both poets are alive.

Although only one poet speaks in the sequence, even when quoting the other, 'Vaughan Variations' reveal both poets. Vaughan the man comes alive through Cluysenaar's response to his work. He is a deeply troubled young man, passionate about religion and politics, and a doctor conscious of his own need of healing. He is an exploratory poet; influenced by George Herbert, but not, like Herbert, a maker of well-controlled verbal forms.[28] In his organic verses he partly finds and partly constructs a self. In this, he is more like Wallace Stevens than Herbert, a poet of 'the poem of the mind in the act of finding / What will suffice'.

The conversation with Vaughan reveals the speaker: her vulnerability, her agony over the disgraces of the age, her thinking about language and its relation to reality, her exploratory art, and her personal relationships. The writing is an

---

27 *The Works of Thomas Vaughan*, p. 52.

28 Even in his dramatically broken poems, such as 'The Collar' and 'Deniall', Herbert is always in control of the form. Vaughan, by contrast, risks appearing disorganized, in poems that are thought-in-process. One would not describe a Herbert poem as Cluysenaar describes Vaughan's 'Distraction': 'a molten flow in which words and experience come simultaneously, both provisional and both, for that very reason, vibrantly alive' (*Scintilla* 1, p. 94).

act of self or soul-making, as Keats would have called it. In his book *The Edge of Words* Rowan Williams says:

> To be aware of oneself *as* a self is to think of a continuing 'conversation' with material data in the course of which . . . the world to which we belong becomes the world that belongs to us.[29]

The phrase 'Material data' recalls Cluysenaar's conception of the human being as 'Matter watching itself',[30] matter becoming self-conscious, and conscious of the animate universe, through language for her, Vaughan's poems were, in this sense, part of the 'material data'. His poems, so alive to the place she came to know and love – the natural, cultural, sacred Welsh landscape – enabled her to belong to that world, and that world to belong to her. Her belonging made no claim to possession or mastery. It was a way of being. The conversation with Vaughan helped her to know herself as a woman and a poet, and as 'a part of reality'.

---

29 Rowan Williams, *The Edge of Words*, Bloomsbury, 2014, p. 73.
30 'Quarry', *Timeslips*, p. 103.

'The River Usk'
by Christopher Werrett

OLIVER MARLOW

Would you grasp a nettle?

Would you grasp a nettle
with teeth round its edge
sharp as a saw?

Whose seeds are like smoke,
whose few grey hairs
are a sign of cancer?

I count to three
and do –
find that it's true:

no pain,

only a view
of valleys from above,
and right down the middle
a stream of light,

as I feel a fly
on my thumb and finger
light as shade
moving over.

School chapel

This morning,
while a man was talking,

saw the different grains
on panels to my right:

first – lines
of bubbles boiling up;

then – a screen
of snow blown across;

last – water,
seen from above,

waves
glinting in the sun.

Inside a church

You come through one door
and opposite is another,
older,
half open,
showing you behind
a wall blocked white.

Come to this door,
up to its wood,
you smell
the last
hints of a Christmas
midnight service;

or,
moving the latch
cold and black
up and down,
you make the sound of the hand of a clock
tick tock

with nowhere to go.
Soon,
you're drawn to the carved
keyhole underneath,
find your finger fits
perfectly,

and,
as if to prove,
the lightest pull
makes it move –
breathe,
until you see behind

and see –
nothing
a wall,
smooth,
a wall so white it shows your shadow
looking back at you

from the other side.
An archway of stone,
white,
blocking the way
big as any boulder.
I wonder.

CAROLINE NATZLER

I Saw

Only a white tree
blossoming with slips of quiet paper
unmarked, lucid beyond thought

and I, thin, lay for once serene
trusting I would never have to scramble back
into the old murk, the scrawls of making sense

trusting I would lift, gather in those slips of clear paper
and bring them home, without words
and bring them home, and they would not be ashes.

Into Life

You longed for a vision
a pattern shining through,

came slowly
to these smears of green and brown
pushed about by a child's fingers.

As If

Stark white walls underscored with dark

filigree of a balcony
written precisely over the bleached ground

so clear cut the shadows

as if the world is pressing itself onto you
harsh with significance

till a flake of withered flower
lifts into a butterfly, scrap of air

the sea like a shawl furling, unfurling along the shore
moves in a length of white paper roll
waving in the breeze of an open window

an arch, dark in a long wall of light
becomes a turret, fierce in the heat hazed sky

and that skittering – a lizard on earth
or the shadow of flight above? –

flowing dark, tipping loose with light
the world reeling.

DOIRAN WILLIAMS

Spring Cleaning

Means taking down the Grandma Moses plate
And the paintings:
Florence from Fiesole,
Women, brollies up, biking through the evening slush
Into an Emilian town,
Light retreating across a Guernsey bay,
A Rhondda hillside before Thatcher,
Savage but alive.
Remove them and you know the feel of loss,
Of bankruptcy, divorce or death,
A stripping of the altar.

Stacked against the chairs they
Turn the room into an artists' commune,
Work by various hands, in
Nantucket, Sark and Richmond Park,
Hard-won milestones, companions, valued
Beyond commerce or insurance,
Not to be dismissed
By those who come after us;
Signs of relationships, our own
And those between ourselves and
All the painters,
Sacraments.

HOWARD WRIGHT

Garden Furniture

THE BIRD TABLE
Shakedown of manna. Menagerie of cats and crows,
nature's raucous anti-thoughts and crumbs
of discomfort from a world beyond ourselves.
I stand my ground while she feeds me words of a song.

THE POND
Listen – the fish are carping about their space.
They are eating me out of house and home.
What they lack in temper they make up for in grace.
I corral them like gold in the depths of the badlands.

THE BIRD BATH
A longer light thickens hedges with calorific glow.
Ants scramble like prospectors, and dogs bark
against themselves. I tremble under flicks of rain
dancing with the very possibility of evening on my skin.

THE ARCH
A master of disguise under sweet pea, honeysuckle
and lilac; the spread of fragrance from the flowerbeds.
Colour is a breath of air, a small beginning with a cast
of thousands; here, flowering corn, there, stock.

THE SUNDIAL
I'm underused, forgotten, a decorative set-square
achingly alert for attention. Overhead, her zenith,
conceited and accurate, she casts no shadow.
By my calculation, there is always time.

THE STATUE
A twisted root, spidery, web-ridden; at the height
of my fame I was a myth, now I'm fake,
a replica cherub, a cheap cement dick flashing
at polite girls on blankets, their faces to the sun.

THE SWING
Slung low like Apollo's chariot, the horses
heave and surge through the trees. I slacken
in the heat, the reins loosen until, swaying
with the effort, I allow the team to graze the clouds.

Hearth and Home

THE FIREGUARD
We are the avant-garde, stomachs jumping
at the skites and implosions, the stiff mesh
distended, shaky, unsteady, fat with smoke
like a chimney-breastplate fixed to a jovial Falstaff
sparking laughter for this love and life.

THE HEARTH
The cat warms its backside like an old man.
The hearth gods are kind. Peace, heat and those
we remember who remembered us for a lifetime.
Then again, a way in for small birds who bounce off
the windows, losing everything the world has to offer.

THE GRATE
Fire-fairies, fauna, crowd goblins; a cloud dictionary.
'Look and Learn'. Belly down, flat out,
engrossed in the antics of Old King Coal,
the upturned beard of Simon Peter kicking his heels
in Rome because of a preacherman from Gallilee.

THE MANTELPIECE
End-of-Empire stuff and a boundless childhood
tinted, crosshatched into a hundred illustrated books.
The big heads of Kitchener, Churchill and Haig
who made high summer a living hell,
the Wade figurines glazed in rigor mortis.

THE FIREPLACE
The tiled stage, props of long brass tongs
and soot-black poker with turned handle, a proscenium
around the roaring chorus of blade-sharp flames,
its audience on the shaggy rug with the rain
dancing outside the ballet of the Child Catcher.

JEREMY YOUNG

Narcissus

The Greeks were mistaken:
you did not fall
in love with your own great beauty
but with the pond's blank
mirror, in which your image
became your whole world,
the woman who loved you
no more than an echo
of your own thoughts.

You did not die
beside the pond pining
for the handsome youth
who broke
into fragments
whenever you reached out
to touch him.

No, you are still alive,
inhabiting a mirror-world
where everyone else
is transformed into a story
about yourself,
and no blow can crack
your liquid looking-glass.

I have known you all my life,
but now when I want to touch you,
your face pours through my fingers
like dry desert sand.

Peter Thomas: A Remembrance

ALAN RUDRUM

What follows is, for various reasons an unsatisfactory version of what I had intended, and less than Peter's memory deserves, both as a person and as a scholar.

I first read Peter's work many years ago, in his wittily titled "Two Cultures? Court and Country Under Charles I", which appeared in 1973 in *The Origins of the English Civil War*, edited by Conrad Russell. A masterpiece of historical learning, and of shrewd analysis, it destroys the underpinnings of conventional wisdom about the period. It begins with a quotation from Dryden's *Absalom and Achitophel* (1679): "And never Rebel was to Arts a friend." Faced with the threat of Monmouth yielding to Shaftesbury's prompting, Dryden recalled the ill effects of "enthusiasm" during the Great Rebellion. In 1682, in the Preface to *Religio Laici*, Dryden carried the quarrel back beyond the Revolution, to Martin Mar-Prelate, and Peter commented that 'this touches deep convictions about politics and literature which we must investigate.'

He goes on to write of the one-sided view we have of Puritanism after the execution of Charles I, his art treasures put up for auction, and theatres closed, 'the great Leviathan of the Republic, presiding grim and godly over a wasteland.' This picture is seen to be one-sided when we consider Marvell, who served the protectorate, and Milton, whose learning and brilliance were a byword in Europe.

Asceticism, then, was not the monopoly of nonconformity; he cites the affinities between the fine spirituality of Richard Baxter and Jeremy Taylor; and the fact that Presbyterians and Independents were 'frequently at one another's throats'. Prynne, Burton, and Lilburne were all Puritans, but they represented in the end quite different points of view.

Jonson's caricature of Puritanism in *Bartholomew Fair*, acted in 1614, printed in 1631, 'expresses the growing anxiety of the early seventeenth century over militant nonconformism.' Peter argues that all the differences, which in the decades prior to Civil War, hardened into faction in 'the challenge of Elizabethan Puritanism . . . and in particular to the controversies of the 1580's.' While the Elizabethan settlement was punitive to extremists, its tolerance of the broad middle rrange of dissent made national unity possible, and is reflected in some

122

of the major literary achievements of the period, notably in Spenser's *Faerie Queene* (1596), written 'to fashion a gentleman or noble person in virtuous and gentle discipline' and celebrating 'that unity of Church and State, of Court with Country . . . that the Queen's Council embodied.'

Especially notable, Peter argues, is Spenser's showing that even the erotic impulse and the language of love songs could serve a holy ideal, as in his celebration of matrimony in *Epithalamion* (1590) 'in which the senses, human feeling, and spiritual fervour triumph together.'

Peter's big book, *Sir John Berkenhead, 1617-1679*, was published in 1969 by the Oxford University Press, 10 years after he submitted it as his Oxford doctoral dissertation, with a dedication to his daughter Simone. I mention this because as I came to know Peter over the years, on several pleasurable and rewarding visits to Wales, his devotion to family became very clear. The first paragraph of his Preface reads: 'Sir John Berkenhead is not one of those victims of time who have sunk without trace: over the centuries biographers, bibliographers, historians of the Press, literary historians, and plain historians have surfaced clutching assorted curious relics (and sometimes larger evidence) of his former fame for wit and loyalty.' It concludes 'There is enough of Berkenhead visible to inspire a larger voyage of recovery.'

In the second paragraph Peter summarises the contribution his book is to make: 'Such an undertaking necessarily begins with the facts of his life and the canon of his works, so many of which were published anonymously. I have brought into view many of the formerly obscure parts of his career, and looked more narrowly at his political and psychological drives than previous biographers. And I have added very considerably to the bulk of work, particularly pamphleteering, attributable to him,' and that this was especially difficult because so much material (jokes, phrases, attitudes and so on) is shared by Royalist propagandists. He adds that in most cases he has invoked corroborative circumstantial evidence.

Berkenhead died in December 1679, and Peter remarks that 'a characteristic circumspection oddly manifested itself: he decreed that his body be laid in the churchyard to prevent its removal from the church itself at some later date when room might be needed for other, presumably more important, cadavers.' Henry Vaughan, whose gentry status would have entitled him to be buried in the church at Llansanffraid, was buried in the churchyard, and the standard interpretation of that is that he decreed it should be so out of humility.

Peter goes on to say that Berkenhead's is the will of a man who found his deepest satisfactions in money and political success, not in literature or the life of the intellect for their own sakes. 'Yet he was not wholly devoid of the softer virtue of gratitude, for his largest bequests (of 40 pounds a year) went to the master of Witton church school which he had attended as a boy and to the minister of his home town. This was tacit recognition that his career, like that of many seventeenth-century office-holders, had advanced through opportunities for "rising" opened up by his education. The other essential for advancement was a powerful patron . . . his great benefactor was Archbishop Laud, into whose mighty orbit he was drawn when, as a youth, he left school and home for Oxford University.'

Peter comments that the Witton Chapel Register shows that Berkenhead's father 'wrote a good italic hand . . . Doubtless Berkenhead acquired his own skill as a scribe from his father. It was to prove an important asset.' Yes indeed, for it was his good handwriting that Laud noticed, as well as the fact that he was temperamentally . . . indisposed to indulge in the debaucheries, common in Oxford at that time, that Laud was keen to stamp out.' When Laud visited the University in August 1936 he 'had occasion to have some things well transcribed, and this Berkenhead . . . performed his businesse so well, that the archbishop recommended him to All Soules' College to be a fellow.' Here I feel that I have lost out, since I have often been congratulated on my penmanship, though some time ago I abandoned the quill and write with a Mont Blanc pen instead. An All Souls fellowship would suit me very well.

On the way to this point Peter clears up a confusion about the date of Berkenhead's birth, which was not at the time recorded in the parish register. Later someone inserted the date of his christening under 24 March 1616, attempting to forge an old hand. The forger's mistake, repeated in the 'Life' in the D.N.B., was probably due to a misunderstanding . . . that he was born on 24 March 1616. This, ignoring the seventeenth-century habit of reckoning the New Year from 25 March, was misinterpreted. 24 March 1617 is the correct date of birth.

Of course I have not compared Peter's dissertation with the book which followed ten years later. What I can say is that he did an amazing amount of research in many different archives, enough to impress other scholars who have got their hands dirty leafing through vellum.

Peter and I became very good friends, as we met on the many visits I made to Vaughan's house, where I was made welcome by the current owners, and where my wife and I, sometimes accompanied by our friend James Carscallen, visited the Priory Grove and trudged around looking for a waterfall that corresponded to the one described in Vaughan's poem. We both liked dogs, and I recall the many times when Peter would unload his two from the back of his car.

Peter, one of the mildest of men, not an ounce of abrasiveness in him, was nevertheless one who set his mind to do something and did not give up until it was done. He had great admiration for Henry Vaughan's poems and a determination to do whatever he could to bring them a wider readership. I had my part in this: in the Tercentenary of Vaughan's death I organized a session on his work at the Modern Languages Association conference and gave a talk on him at another session; and I crossed the Atlantic twice to read papers on Vaughan in Wales. It was at a talk in the Brecon public library that it became clear that a great many in the audience were not professional scholars at all, but lay persons who were interested in his poems. It was then that I remarked that working on Vaughan had been a somewhat lonely business, and that it was heartening to see that a great many others were interested in his poems. So it would be good to have an association devoted to the work of the Vaughans. This was taken up by others, notably by Peter and Anne Cluysenar. And so the Usk Valley Vaughan Association was formed and *Scintilla* was born. Anne was the first General Editor, with an editorial board of six people. By *Scintilla's* third issue, Peter had become the General Editor. It had financial support from the Arts Council of Wales and the University of Wales, Cardiff. Its production values were, and remained, very high, with beautiful art-work and poems that in many cases, without imitating Vaughan, had affinities with his work.

Donald Dickson, Robert Wilcher and Glyn Pursglove became contributors and Jonathan Nauman, a private scholar in America, contributed and also attended the annual conferences of the Association. The result was that more scholarly and critical attention was paid to the Vaughans during the years of *Scintilla* than during the previous fifty, and the annual bibliographies of *PMLA*, with its records of articles on Vaughan in other learned journals, might well represent a greater awareness of Vaughan brought about by those in *Scintilla*.

Among the many distinguished contributors to *Scintilla* we find Donald Allchin, Roland Mathias, Stevie Davies, Peter Thomas's wonderful article on 'The Language of Light: Henry Vaughan and the Puritans,' Seamus Heaney, Les Murray, Brigid Allen's important essay 'The Vaughans at Jesus College' in *Scintilla* 4 , Rowan Williams in numbers 7, 8 and 15 (an essay and two poems), and Philip West, author of the excellent book 'Henry Vaughan's *Silex Scintillans*, Scripture Uses' and now a Fellow of Somerville College Oxford, in numbers 9 and 18. "Here be God's plenty."

Then, there is the not-so-little matter of the annual conferences. Having been the principal organizer for two conferences myself, I am aware of the extraordinary amount of work and complexity involved, rather as if one had to run a hotel by oneself, single-handed. So, in thinking of Peter, we should also recall the amount of work that he and Anne put into those occasions, how enjoyable they were, how good the food was, compared to that at the 'banquets' of other organizations, and how grateful most of us surely were for the opportunity to wander over the Brecon Beacons, to see Tretower Court and the many aspects of Vaughan's world that this enabled.

One of the saddest aspects of old age is the loss of our friends, and I miss Peter greatly.

CONTRIBUTORS

MARIA APICHELLA completed her PhD at Aberystwyth University. An award winning poet, her first full collection *Psalmody* won Eyewear's Melita Hume Prize. Her pamphlet *Paga* was published by Cinnamon Press (2015). She teaches at The University of Maryland, Europe.

JOSEPH ASHMORE is studying for a PhD in English at Pembroke College, Cambridge. His doctoral research is investigating the relationship between scriptural hermeneutics and epistemology in early modern religious writing. The thesis will include chapters on Lancelot Andrewes, Sir Thomas Browne, and Henry Vaughan.

MATTHEW BARTON has published two collections, with Peterloo and Brodie Press. His third is forthcoming from Shoestring in the spring. He teaches poetry at Oxford and is co-editor of the poetry magazine *Raceme* (www.racemepoetry.com).

RUTH BIDGOOD lives in mid-Wales. She has twice been short-listed for Wales Book of the Year, and won the Roland Mathias Prize in 2011. A new collection of her poems is due from Cinnamon Press this year.

PRUE CHAMBERLAYNE's poetry pursues her unlived life, nourished by a Severn childhood, rural and mountainous France, and links with Uganda after a career in teaching and biographical research.

WILLIAM VIRGIL DAVIS is a widely published and award-winning poet and critic. His most recent book is *Dismantlements of Silence: Poems Selected and New* (2015).

JOHN FREEMAN's collections include *White Wings: New and Selected Prose Poems* (Contraband Books), *A Suite for Summer*(Worple), and *The Light Is Of Love, I Think: New and Selected Poems* (Stride). He taught for many years at Cardiff University.

MARC HARSHMAN's second full-length poetry collection, *Believe What You Can*, is forthcoming from West Virginia University. His thirteenth book for children, *One Big Family*, has just been published by Eerdmans. He is the poet laureate of West Virginia.

GRAHAM HARTILL worked for several years alongside Anne Cluysenaar and Hilary Llewellyn-Williams as a poetry editor for *Scintilla*. His latest collection is *Chroma*, published by Hafan Books.

JEREMY HOOKER's most recent books are *Openings: A European Journal* and *Scattered Light* (poems). He is Emeritus Professor of English of the University of South Wales, and a Fellow of The Welsh Academy and The Learned Society of Wales.

ROSIE JACKSON lives near Frome, Somerset. Her books include *Fantasy: The Literature of Subversion, Frieda Lawrence* and *Mothers Who Leave*. Poetry Salzburg published *What the Ground Holds* in 2014, and her first full collection *The Light Box*, comes out with Cultured Llama in 2016. *The Glass Mother*, a memoir, also appears in 2016 from Unthank Books.

OLIVER MARLOW has had poems published in several anthologies including *New Poetries II* (Carcanet Press, editor Michael Schmidt). He is working towards his first collection.

CAROLINE NATZLER's poetry collections are *Design Fault* (Flambard Press 2001), *Smart Dust* (Grenadine Press 2009), *Fold* (Hearing Eye 2014) and *Only* (Grenadine Press 2015). She teaches creative writing at the City Lit in London and also runs free-lance workshops.

JONATHAN NAUMAN, Secretary of the Vaughan Association (USA), has a chapter on "Vaughan and Nature" forthcoming in *Henry Vaughan and the Usk Valley* (Logaston Press, 2016), and an essay entitled "Chesterton's Chalk: Creativity and the Commonplace in J. R. R. Tolkien's 'On Fairy-stories'" forthcoming in *Hither Shore*.

ALAN RUDRUM was born in Great Yarmouth, England, on 30th November 1932 and was evacuated at the age of seven, with his sister, aged five, to a farming family in Farndon. He saw his father only once in the next four years. Educated at King's College, London and Cambridge University, he taught at the University of Adelaide, Queen's University, Belfast, the University of California and Kent State University before moving to Simon Fraser University. He is currently working with two associate editors on an edition of *The Complete Works of Henry Vaughan* for the Oxford University Press.

JOSEPH STERRETT is Associate Professor of English Literature at Aarhus University and General Editor of *Scintilla*. His previous books are *The Unheard Prayer: Religious Toleration in Shakespeare's Drama* and *Sacred Text-Sacred Space: Architectural, Spiritual and Literary Convergences in England and Wales* co-edited with Peter Thomas. A new book, *Prayer and Performance: Gesture, Word and Devotion in the Literature of Early Modern England* is imminent.

ROBERT WILCHER retired some years ago as Reader in Early Modern Studies in the English Department at the University of Birmingham and is now an honorary Fellow of the Shakespeare Institute in Stratford-upon-Avon. His publications include *Andrew Marvell* (CUP, 1985), *The Writing of Royalism 1628-1660* (CUP, 2001), *The Discontented Cavalier: The Work of Sir John Suckling in its Social, Religious, Political, and Literary Contexts* (University of Delaware Press, 2007), and essays on Shakespeare, seventeenth-century poetry, *Eikon Basilike*, and modern drama. He is one of three editors working on a complete works of Henry Vaughan for Oxford University Press and has recently co-edited *Henry Vaughan and the Usk Valley* (Logaston Press, 2016).

DOIRAN WILLIAMS was born in North Wales of Welsh parents. After the army he joined the government legal service. On retirement he was ordained an Anglican priest and lives in Hereford diocese.

HOWARD WRIGHT lectures in Art History at the Belfast School of Art, Ulster University. His first collection, *King of Country* was published by Blackstaff in 2010. Recent poems have appeared in the Honest Ulsterman, The Fiddlehead and Cyphers. He also read at the John Hewitt Summer School in Armagh City last July.

JEREMY YOUNG's poetry has been widely published. His pamphlet, *The Wind's Embrace* was published in 2014 as Acumen Occasional Pamphlets No. 24. He lives in Somerset and works in private practice as a Systemic Family Therapist.

FEATURED ARTIST

With this memorial issue for Peter Thomas, we thought it appropriate to invite Christopher Werrett, Peter's grandson, to photograph places in and around the Usk Valley that he had visited when young. Christopher is studying Cinema and Photography at the University of Leeds and was keen to revisit the area to capture some of the landscapes which played such an important part in the lives of his Grandfather and the metaphysical poet, Henry Vaughan. He can be contacted at me@cwphotographics.com.

The cover image is *Tall Waterfall*.

Made in the USA
Charleston, SC
14 April 2016